Contents

Acknowledgments

We would like to acknowledge and thank Chan Chap Choi, Jasper for his computing skills.

New Ways in Teaching Listening

David Nunan and Lindsay Miller, Editors

New Ways in TESOL Series

Innovative Classroom Techniques

Jack C. Richards, Series Editor

Teachers of English to Speakers of Other Languages, Inc.

Typeset in Garamond Book and Tiffany Demi
by Automated Graphic Systems, White Plains, Maryland, USA
and printed by
Pantagraph Printing, Bloomington, Illinois USA

Teachers of English to Speakers of Other Languages, Inc.
700 South Washington Street, Suite 200
Alexandria, Virginia 22314 USA
Tel 703-836-0774 • Fax 703-836-7864 • E-mail tesol@tesol.org • http//www.tesol.org/

Director of Communications and Marketing: Helen Kornblum
Senior Editor: Marilyn Kupetz
Copy Editor: Ellen Garshick
Cover Design: Capitol Communication Systems, Inc., Crofton, Maryland, USA
Part Title Illustrations: David Connell

ISBN 0-939791-58-7
Library of Congress Catalogue No. 94-061423

Introduction

Listening is assuming greater and greater importance in many foreign language contexts, which have until relatively recently focused their efforts on the development of writing skills. This growing importance is reflected in the proliferation of commercial listening courses.

The importance of listening in second and foreign language learning is admirably summarized in a recent publication by Rost (1994):

1. Listening is vital in the language classroom because it provides input for the learner. Without understanding input at the right level, any learning simply cannot begin.
2. Spoken language provides a means of interaction for the learner. Because learners must interact to achieve understanding, access to speakers of the language is essential. Moreover, learners' failure to understand the language they hear is an impetus, not an obstacle, to interaction and learning.
3. Authentic spoken language presents a challenge for the learner to attempt to understand language as native speakers actually use it.
4. Listening exercises provide teachers with a means for drawing learners' attention to new forms (vocabulary, grammar, new interaction patterns) in the language. (pp. 141-142)

In short, listening is essential not only as a receptive skill but also to the development of spoken language proficiency.

This original collection of practical ideas for new ways of teaching listening reflects Rost's perspectives on listening. The book contains contributions from all corners of the globe, from practicing classroom teachers. They point to the growing maturity of the profession and the value to the field of garnering ideas for teaching from those places specifically constituted to bring about teaching and learning, that is, classrooms. One of the reasons we have confidence in the ideas set out here is that they have passed the critical test: They work in the classroom.

Part I focuses on cognitive strategies. The first of these, and one that commonly forms the point of departure for listening work, is listening for the main ideas. This is followed by a section setting out tasks designed to give students practice in listening for details. The third section on cognitive listening strategies deals with predicting.

Following these three sets of strategy-oriented tasks, Part II contains activities that demonstrate the interlinked nature of language skills. These deal respectively with listening and speaking, listening and pronunciation, and listening and vocabulary. A key point in the quotation from Rost is the importance of listening to the general development of oral language. Not surprisingly, therefore, the book contains a collection of tasks featuring both listening and speaking.

The following section provides practical ideas for teaching aspects of stress, intonation, and register. The tasks underline the close relationship between listening and pronunciation. The next section sets out ideas for teaching vocabulary through listening tasks. The tasks present a wide variety of techniques for facilitating vocabulary acquisition through active listening.

The two essential ingredients in any listening task are some form of aural stimulus that provides a point of departure for the task and, second, a set of operations that the learners perform on the task. As Rost makes clear, the use of authentic data is an important element in encouraging the development of listening in a foreign language. In putting this collection together, we were therefore very pleased that a substantial number of contributions took authentic data as their point of departure. We have created a separate section for these tasks (Part III) to highlight the importance of authentic input data in developing listening skills.

Part IV deals with the use of technology in the listening classroom. Although not all teachers will have access to the necessary hardware for experimenting with all of the tasks, the majority are sufficiently "low tech" to be usable in all but the most difficult of teaching contexts.

Part V contains contributions that focus on the area of listening for academic purposes. This area is crucial for teachers at universities and colleges, where a substantial amount of the input to learners is in a language other than their first. These tasks are lively and interesting in their own right and we hope all teachers, not only those working in college contexts, will take a look at them.

Part VI draws together a disparate series of tasks that all deal with affective aspects of the listening process: tasks that take songs as their point of departure and tasks designed for relaxing students.

An Addendum includes tasks designed for dealing with and, in some cases, preempting problems in the listening classroom.

This collection contains a rich array of tasks for teaching listening comprehension.We believe that they are useful and usable in a wider variety of contexts and situations. We also believe that they demonstrate a crucially important fact of classroom life: that the building blocks of the curriculum, there they are the so-called macroskills of listening, speaking, reading, and writing or the linguistic elements of grammar, phonetics, and vocabulary, do not exists independently and should not be taught in isolation. Although the major focus of the tasks in this collection is listening, they all draw on, exploit, and develop other skills as well. Listening is presented separately in this collection for pedagogical convenience. It is up to you, the classroom professional, to sequence and integrate these tasks into your curriculum so that they are in harmony with the development of all the skills.

Reference

Rost, M. (1994). *Introducing listening.* London: Penguin.

Users' Guide to Activities

Part I: Developing Cognitive Strategies

Listening for the Main Idea

Listening for Details

Predicting

Part II: Developing Listening With Other Skills

Listening and Speaking

Part III: Listening to Authentic Material

Part IV: Using Technology

Part V: Listening for Academic Purposes

Part VI: Listening for Fun

Addendum: Planning and Troubleshooting

Part I: Developing Cognitive Strategies

◆ Listening for the Main Idea Listening Task for Narrated Stories

Levels
Any

Aims
Enjoy listening closely
to a story
Develop interest in a
story
Interact in groups
Consolidate pretaught
vocabulary

Class Time
20–30 minutes

Preparation Time
15 minutes

Resources
Narrated story such as
those found in *What a
Story!* (1976)
Blank cards

The teacher can easily manipulate this task to consolidate various lexical items.

Procedure

1. Select an interesting listening passage and write key words and phrases on pieces of card. Make enough sets of cards for groups of three.
2. Preteach the new vocabulary that appears on the cards.
3. Tell students that they are going to listen to a story and that key words and phrases from the story are on the cards. Distribute sets to groups of three.
4. In groups, have students sequence the cards to make the skeleton of a story. Ask a spokesperson from each group to tell the story to the rest of the class.
5. Play the story to the students, who reorder theirs as necessary.
6. Check that the cards have been reordered correctly and ask whether any group had the correct order before listening to the story from the tape.

References and Further Reading

Underwood, M. (1976). *What a Story!* Oxford: Oxford University Press.

Contributor

William Bickerdike is Senior Teacher at the British Council, Riyadh, Saudia Arabia.

Another Way to Say It

Levels
High intermediate +

Aims
Recognize variations of
language functions
Practice paraphrasing

Class Time
10–15 minutes

Preparation Time
30–45 minutes

Resources
VCR
Prepared sheets, one
per student/group

Students need to develop a repertoire of language functions in order to expand their sociolinguistic competence in English.

Procedure

1. Videotape a short clip of any sitcom or select a short clip from a movie. The clip should contain extensive dialogue (as opposed to an action sequence) showing a wide variety of language functions.
2. Select 10–15 language functions in the clip and write paraphrases in large letters on typing paper. The paraphrases may show a change in register (formal/informal/neutral).
3. Show the clip with no preteaching. Have the students provide feedback on possible relationships between the actors and on the general situation (where/when/what).
4. Pass out one paraphrase sheet per student and instruct the class to listen to the clip, again for the language that most closely matches the paraphrase. Students respond by holding up their sheets when the phrases match.
5. As a follow-up activity, write the original phrases on the board and ask the students to tape the paraphrases next to the corresponding phrases. The class could then discuss register, tone of language, or appropriateness to various situations or role-play the situation, with each group choosing a different register.

Caveats and Options

Following the initial viewing of the clip, write five or six sentences from the dialogue on the board and ask students to offer their own paraphrases. Then classify the language produced as formal/informal/neutral/slang, and so forth.

Contributor

Dennis Bricault teaches at North Park College, in Chicago, in the United States.

4

A Famous Explorer

Levels
Beginning

Aims
Follow a simple oral
narrative by developing
sequencing skills

Class Time
15 minutes

Preparation Time
15–30 minutes

Resources
Short, taped narrative
account of a famous
explorer taken from the
class text or devised by
the teacher
Copies of the route the
explorer took on his
journey
A table of events

This exercise is useful where English is being used to simultaneously teach other curricular areas, such as geography. It can also be used as a basis for a guided writing task in which students become familiar with sequencing markers such as *first, then, after that*, and *a few years later*.

Procedure

1. Elicit from the students what they know about the explorer in question.
2. Play the tape of the explorer's adventure. Have students trace the route of the explorer's journey on an simple map, check their route with a partner, and listen to the tape again.
3. Distribute a table of events with sequence markers in the correct order but with the events jumbled up. Have the students' listen to the tape again and arrange the events in the correct order by drawing lines on the table. The table may look something like the following:

	Event
First,	arrived in Cairo
Then,	took boat to Luxor
After that,	started journey from Paris

4. As a follow-up exercise, have students write a paragraph about the explorer from their notes and map.

Caveats and Options

Leave the table of events blank and have students listen to the tape and write their own short notes for each event.

Contributor

Dominic Cogan is a Lecturer in English at Fukui Prefectural University, Japan. Previously, he has worked in TESOL in Ireland, Ghana, and Oman.

What's for Sale?

Levels
Intermediate

Aims
Develop the ability to
gather information
Draw conclusions from
aural information
through a game format

Class Time
10–15 minutes

Preparation Time
10 minutes

Resources
Recording of a TV
advertisement that does
not name the product in
the soundtrack

This activity teaches students to realize the importance of information gathering in order to draw conclusions or make informal judgments.

Procedure

1. Explain to the students that they are going to play a game, the purpose of which is to gather as much information as possible. Remind the students that it is important to collect as much information as they can so that they can come to realistic, accurate conclusions and decisions.
2. Divide the class into pairs of A and B.
3. Have the Bs turn away from the screen and listen only to the soundtrack while the As watch the video.
4. Have partners face each other.
5. Have the Bs ask yes/no questions like the ones below about the TV advertisement for a set time. Each Yes answer gains B a point, and each No answer gains A a point.

    Were there any people in the ad? Yes
    Were there many people in the ad? No

6. In the final 10 seconds, have the Bs guess what was being advertised. The As either reject or confirm the guess.
7. Show the advertisement again and have all the students watch both the visuals and hear the soundtrack.
8. Award the Bs who guessed correctly 5 points. If someone from B group guesses incorrectly, their A partner gets the 5 points.
9. Calculate marks and reveal the scores.

Caveats and Options

Have the Bs make true/false statements instead of asking yes/no questions if it is more appropriate to the language focus or level of the class.

Contributor

Geraldine Hetherton is currently working as an ESOL teacher in Japan. She has also taught ESOL in Ireland, Ghana, and Oman.

Folk and Fairy Tales: Enjoying a Story

Levels
Any

Aims
Develop understanding
and appreciation
(affective processing)

Class Time
15–25 minutes

Preparation Time
10 minutes

Resources
A tape or script of a
folk or fairy tale
Copies of a story
skeleton (plot outline)
of the story
Overhead projector

Learners are often asked to do fairly concrete, literal comprehension tasks. However, literal comprehension is only one—and usually the lowest—level of comprehension. This activity encourages learners to process a story at a higher level.

Procedure

1. Choose a folk or fairy tale that learners are unlikely to know. It should be one that students are likely to have an emotional response to. For this reason, scary stories—in some cultures, the type people tell around campfires late at night, work very well.
2. Prepare a story skeleton either on handouts for the learners or on an overhead projector transparency.
3. In class, give the learners the skeleton. Tell the story as the students follow the skeleton.
4. After they listen, write the following on the board:

   Was the story interesting? Why or why not?
   Was it scary (funny, exciting . . .)? Why or why not?

5. Have learners give their own reactions to the story in groups of two to four.

Caveats and Options

1. At lower levels, you may want to allow the last step to be in the learners' L1. Because listening is receptive, it may be unrealistic to expect discussion (a productive skill) in English.
2. At first glance, this activity may appear to lack a clear task. However, having to state one's reaction is actually a task that indicates a very

sophisticated level of understanding. If your learners need a more concrete goal, specify a minimum number of sentences they must use (at least three).

3. Defining *appreciation* as the highest level of comprehension is based on Barrett's taxonomy of reading comprehension (from lowest to highest): (a) literal understanding, (b) reorganization, (c) inference, (d) evaluation, and (e) appreciation.

References and Further Reading

Barrett, T. C. (1986) What is reading? In T. Clymer (Ed.), *Innovation and change in reading instruction. 67th Year Book of the National Society for Study of Education,* University of Chicago Press.

Contributors

Marc Helgesen is Associate Professor at Miyagi Gakuin Women's College, Sendai Japan. Steven Brown is Curriculum Coordinator at the University of Pittsburgh English Language Institute in the United States. They are coauthors of the Active Listening series (Cambridge University Press) and the New English Firsthand series (Longman/Lingual House).

Jigsaw Listening: A Lesson

Levels
Intermediate +

Aims
Practice finding the
main idea
Predict information

Class Time
1 1/2 hours

Preparation Time
25 minutes

Resources
Two short taped
passages of interest to
your students
Separate lists of
questions for each
passage (written by the
teacher)

This listening gap exercise reinforces the idea that listening is an integral part of communication.

Procedure

1. Divide the class into two groups.
2. Send each group to a tape recorder and ask them to listen to the passage for as long as needed. Each group will listen to a different passage. They should then write down 15 words (or phrases) that are the key words in the passage. Tell them that these ideas should represent the most important ideas in the passage. (It is helpful if they have already worked on this skill in either listening or reading.)
3. Have each group write their 15 key words on their half of the board.
4. Have the two groups move to opposite sides of the room so that they are facing the key words to the passage they have not listened to.
5. Have students in each group read the key words on the board in front of them and predict/guess what the listening passage (that they have not heard yet) is about. Encourage the students to discuss this within their group.
6. Ask each group to discuss among themselves and then say out loud what they think the passage they haven't listened to is about. (Remember, the other half of the class has heard the other passage.) Don't let any "answers" be given at this time. This is just a time for listening to students' predictions.
7. Give the students a list of questions on the passage they haven't listened to. Ask the students to try to answer the questions from their predictions of the passage.
8. Tell the students to find a partner from the other group. The partners will ask each other questions from their list (Step 7), but they cannot

show the other person their list of questions. The information they have gained from listening to the passages has become the basis for a communication gap exercise. At this point each student should know the answers to the other student's questions as he has listened to the other passage several times. However, it is possible that the student will not have the answers.

9. Have the students go back to their original groups and exchange information about the passage they haven't heard. (This step can be deleted if you have a short class period.)
10. Let the students listen to the tape they haven't heard.
11. Discuss the two lists of questions with the teacher and the whole group.
12. Hand out the tapescript.

Caveats and Options

1. Instead of two passages, use two halves of a story (one group has the first half and the other group has the second half.)
2. Use two versions of the same story and have the students find similarities and differences.

Contributor

Jean Jewell is Assistant Director of the English for Art Program at the Academy of Art College, San Francisco, California, in the United States.

Hear All About It

Levels
Intermediate

Aims
Develop skill in
listening for topic
markers

Class Time
15 minutes

Preparation Time
30 minutes

Resources
Two sets of short,
taped radio news
bulletins broadcast on
the same day from two
different radio stations,
such as a national or
local radio station and
the BBC or Voice of
America

The radio provides a valuable source of authentic listening material. This activity gives students confidence in listening to broadcasts in English on the radio.

Procedure

1. Tell students that they are going to listen to two short news bulletins.
2. On the board, write a topic name for each news story contained in both bulletins. Some examples follow:

   International trade agreement
   Nobel Peace Prize award
   Floods in Bangladesh
   AIDS statistics
   Airplane crash
   Royal family scandal

3. Tell students that these are the news stories covered in both news bulletins. Make sure that the news story topics are ordered differently than they are in the bulletins. Discuss any vocabulary in the list that may be unknown to your students (e.g., *scandal*).
4. Tell your students that the order of news items presented may not be the same in each bulletin and that some news items may appear in one bulletin but not in the other. Tell the students that you will play each news bulletin once and that their task is to make a list of the news items in the order that they are presented in the two separate columns.
5. Play the first news bulletin. Allow students to check their news story ordering in pairs. Play the second news bulletin. Allow the students

to check their ordering and compare it with that of the news stories in the first bulletin.

6. Elicit the ordering of news stories for both news bulletins and write them on the board. Discuss the differences on order, and discuss which news stories were included in one bulletin but not the other. Discuss which key words helped the students select the news topic heading.

Caveats and Options

For high intermediate classes, do not write all the news story topic headings on the board. Instead, distribute a handout with only some of the news story topic headings for each bulletin:

News Bulletin 1:

1. International trade agreement   4. Nobel Peace Prize

2. _____   5. _____

3. _____   6. _____

News Bulletin 2:

1. _____   4. _____

2. Nobel Peace Prize   5. AIDS statistics

3. Floods in Bangladesh   6. _____

Contributor

Dino Mahoney has lived and taught in Europe, the Middle East, and the Far East. He was Director of Studies for the British Council in Dubai and Hong Kong.

A Soap Opera

Levels
Intermediate +

Aims
Listen to a story for
pleasure
Follow a story line

Class Time
40 minutes

Preparation Time
Varies

Resources
Chalkboard

Storytelling is a major part of Western culture. Many people watch soap operas as part of their everyday lives. This activity capitalizes on the essential features of soap operas: a story line with a cliff-hanging ending.

Procedure

1. At the beginning of a course, discuss with the students what their favorite soap operas are. Have the students give a short account of the story, characters, and themes of the soap opera.
2. Inform the class that they are going to make up their own soap opera. Begin by brainstorming ideas for the soap opera (this could be done in small groups first). Have students think of the characters, where they live, their jobs, their relationships, and so forth.
3. For the next class, prepare a short story based on the ideas generated in class. Try to introduce the characters and the beginning of a story line. Leave the ending vague.
4. Divide the class into groups of three or four. Chose one group and tell them that they have to write the next episode of the story for the next class using the characters already introduced and leaving the ending vague or in suspense.
5. At the next lesson ask the group to read out their episode (you may want to set a standard length for each episode, e.g., four pages) while the rest of the class listens carefully. The students should not take notes but rather listen and try to remember what has happened.
6. Choose another group to prepare the next episode for the following lesson. This practice can continue until the end of the course or until everyone decides that the plot has gone on long enough and a new soap opera is required.

15

Caveats and Options

Ask the students to submit their episode for review before they read it to the class. You can then suggest ways to improve the plot and/or English.

Contributor

Lindsay Miller is a Lecturer in the English Department of the City University of Hong Kong. He has taught EFL in Europe, the Middle East, and Southeast Asia.

What's My Job?

Levels
Elementary–low
intermediate

Aims
Hear more than
understand
Learn about the topic of
jobs

Class Time
5–10 minutes

Preparation Time
10 minutes

Resources
Several written
paragraphs describing
various jobs with clues
as to the job but
without the name of the
job, recorded on tape if
desired

At low levels, language teachers usually try to control the language input. This activity begins to prepare students to listen to language at a higher level than they can understand.

Procedure

1. Write the topic of the lesson on the board: jobs, for example. Ask your students about some of the jobs they have had.
2. Tell the class that they are going to hear some information about different jobs. Tell them that they might not understand all the words and that the speaker will speak fast. All they have to do is listen and write down the name of the job when they think they know it.
3. Read the descriptions, or play the tape, to the class (see Appendix). At the end of each description ask the students what the job is.
4. Have the students tell you any words in the description that helped them know what job was being described. Write the words on the board and have the students listen again to the description to see if they can hear them.
5. Write any words the students think they heard, but did not, and ask them to listen again and check if all the words on the board are in the description.

Appendix: Sample Job Description

I usually work during the day but sometimes at night as well. The nights are better as it is quieter on the streets. I meet a lot of people, some nice, some not so nice. I prefer older people as they talk to me, and when you drive around all day it's nice to have a chat with someone. It's really expensive to hire my car, and the cost of petrol is going up and up, so I've got to work hard to earn a living. I think

I'll have to stop driving soon as the stress is too much. Maybe I'll go back to my village and be a farmer again. (The job is taxi driver.)

Contributor

Lindsay Miller is a Lecturer in the English Department at the City University of Hong Kong. He has taught EFL in Europe, the Middle East, and Southeast Asia.

Classroom Instructions

Levels
Beginning

Aims
Concentrate on in-class listening
Understand classroom instructions

Class Time
5–10 minutes

Preparation Time
10 minutes

Resources
None

Changing classroom instructions from day to day gives the students much more practice in listening to instructions, and adds variety to the class schedule.

Procedure

At some point during class each day, announce some special instruction for the next day's class. Offer a special reward for those that follow the instruction correctly. Some examples are:

Tomorrow we will meet in the lobby rather than in the classroom.

Tomorrow we will only have chairs for the first 10 students to arrive in class. The others will have to stand.

Tomorrow anyone who wears something blue to class will have to sing a song.

Tomorrow there will be a test for anyone who arrives on time. Everyone who arrives 5 minutes late will play a game.

Caveats and Options

Keep a sense of humor about this activity. Students should feel embarrassed enough to concentrate on listening, but not become ashamed or humiliated. Usually no consequence should last more than 5 minutes.

Contributor

Hugh Rutledge graduated from Boston University in 1988. He has taught in East Asia for several years and is Head of Faculty at Tokyo International Collge in Japan.

Listen to My Story

Levels
Low intermediate +

Aims
Practice listening to long stretches of discourse
Link listening and speaking through the relaying of a story

Class Time
1 hour +

Preparation Time
30 minutes–1 hour

Resources
Several short stories of interest to your students
Audiotapes of the stories
As many tape recorders as you have groups

To enhance their concentration span, learners must have the opportunity to follow long stretches of spoken discourse that is free from too great a lexical density and that describes events and human reactions rather than abstract arguments. A story with a clear chronological sequence of factual events and containing a suspense element is ideal for this.

Procedure

1. Make notes on the stories and use the notes to record the stories, one per tape.
2. Arrange the class into groups of 8-10. Give each group a taped story and a tape recorder. Try to arrange for the groups to work in different rooms so that they do not interrupt each other.
3. Tell the students to listen to the story as many times as they like. (Put student in charge of controlling the tape recorder.) The task is to understand the story as completely as they can. Have students (a) take no notes, (b) make their own notes, (c) make their own notes and compile them into notes for the group, (d) use a teacher-provided skeleton outline of the story.
4. After a predetermined time, or once everyone in the group feels confident that they know the story, bring the students together and pair them up or form small groups so that each group has someone in it who can tell a different story. Allow the students to tell each other their stories.

Caveats and Options

1. Some of Roald Dahl's stories are suitable, but traditional folk tales are also good sources, as are extracts from history books and biographies.

2. Forgo cassettes and simply tell the story separately to the groups. (The group in the other room will be doing some unrelated task.)
3. Before the whole class reconvenes, have students retell the story to each other with echoing or shadowing, that is, one student tells a short section of the story, the other recapitulates.
4. Have the students work in a language laboratory and record all the stories they heard on tape. Then they can rewind, listen to themselves and try to retell the story to make it sound more interesting, by focusing on the prosodic features of their speech.

Contributor

Richard J. Shorter is Associate Professor of English at Nagoya Gakuin University, Seto-shi, Aichi-ken, Japan.

◆ Listening for Details Around the World

Levels
Intermediate

Aims
Practice peer-focused listening

Class Time
15–20 minutes/student presentation

Preparation Time
30 minutes

Resources
Atlas
Almanac
Individual copies of a world map
Crayons or colored markers

A structured listening task helps students to focus when a peer is addressing the class. When a standardized speaking/listening format is used for multiple presentations, students gain confidence from the additional listening practice and learn to listen as they would have others listen to them.

Procedure

1. Create a simple worksheet to serve as the basis for oral presentations as well as a parallel listening task:

   Country _____
   Capital _____
   Language(s) _____
   Size _____
   Population _____
   States or Provinces _____
   Climate _____
   Government _____
   Culture _____
   (food, clothing, music, customs)
   Flag _____

2. Model the oral presentation. Distribute the above worksheet to each student or have students copy it from the board. Present information on your country or elicit it from the class. Encourage clarification questions as students complete their worksheets.

3. Explain the purpose and strategy of the activity. Students will work individually or in pairs or groups to prepare a presentation on their countries or a country of their choice. There will be one presentation

per day. Listening students will identify each day's country on their world map and complete a new worksheet by writing the information that they hear. Students will assemble their information sheets into a booklet, a tangible product of their listening skills.

4. Allow preparation time. Groups and pairs from the same country should organize by deciding who will cover what part of the presentation. Individuals who are the sole representative of their country can work alone or team up with someone from a kindred country. Students can research size and population figures in the almanac or atlas you have provided. They can ignore or elaborate any aspect of the culture segment.

5. Participate as a learner. Join the students in completing an information sheet for each presentation. Focus your listening on individual oral habits.

Caveats and Options

1. Use cassettes to record the presentations.
2. Follow up with an exercise of student-generated questions. (e.g., Which countries have the same climate?)
3. Try the same technique with a different topic (e.g., students fill out a chart while students take turns introducing a classmate they have interviewed.)

Contributor

Joan Blankmann teaches adult ESOL and English for occupational purposes for Fairfax County, Virginia, in the United States. She also teaches at the Annandale campus of Northern Virginia Community College.

Finding Mr. Right

Levels
Beginning

Aims
Ask and respond to
questions about
personal information
Practice yes/no
questions and short
answers, personal
descriptions, ages, and
possessives

Class Time
5–10 minutes

Preparation Time
10–15 minutes

Resources
Handout, notebook
paper, chalkboard, or
overhead projector

In this activity students need to keep asking a short series of questions in order to find someone who meets a set of criteria.

Procedure

1. Prepare a sheet with two lists: the first with several personal relationships (e.g., mother, brother, friend, roommate) and the second with number of personal characteristics (e.g., tall, short, young, intelligent, rich). Copy and hand out the lists, or write the lists on the board and have the students copy them onto a sheet of notebook paper (see Appendix A).
2. Ask the students to circle any one relationship and any three adjectives.
3. Review two questions to ask and their answers:

   Do you have (a brother)? Yes, I do.
   Is he (tall)? No, he isn't.

4. Have students look for a classmate who can answer yes to all four questions, the first about the relationship, the others about the characteristics. If students are unable to find the desired person, they can choose another trait. Appendix B shows a flow chart to put on the board or overhead projector as a guide to the students.
5. As a follow-up in class, have students report back about the person found. Time permitting, classmates can check off the characteristics heard during this stage.

Caveats and Options

Extend the descriptive portion of the sheet to other lexical fields, such as likes/dislikes, or hobbies.

Appendix A: Sample Worksheet

Búsqueda (Search)

1. Choose one relationship:

padre	*madre*	*hermano*	*hermana*
amigo	*amiga*	*abuelo*	*abuela*
compañero de cuarto		*esposo*	*esposa*
compañera de cuarto		*hijo*	*hija*
compañero de clase		*novio*	*novia*
compañera de clase			

2. Choose three traits:

delgado/a	*gordo/a*	*anciano/a*
guapo/a	*feo/a*	*bajo/a*
alto/a	*atlético/a*	*atractivo/a*
joven	*inteligente*	*paciente*
rubio	*moreno*	*pelirrojo*
simpático	*antipático*	

3. Now look for a classmate who has a friend/relative with these personal traits by asking these questions.

   Relación: *¿Tienes ....?* _____
   Características: *¿Es ....?* _____ _____ _____

4. Report back to the class:

   (Luis) tiene una hermana. Es alta, guapa, y joven. Se llama (Juana). Ella tiene 20 años. Su dirección es ....

Appendix B: Flow Chart

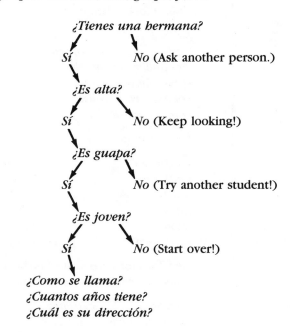

Ejemplo: hermana; alta, guapa, joven

¿Tienes una hermana?

Sí   *No* (Ask another person.)

¿Es alta?

Sí   *No* (Keep looking!)

¿Es guapa?

Sí   *No* (Try another student!)

¿Es joven?

Sí   *No* (Start over!)

¿Como se llama?
¿Cuantos años tiene?
¿Cuál es su dirección?

Contributor

Dennis Bricault teaches at North Park College, Chicago, in the United States.

Content Listening Cloze Exercise

Levels
Beginning +

Aims
Listen for content or meaning

Class Time
20–25 minutes

Preparation Time
20 minutes

Resources
Passage appropriate for the proficiency level
Overhead projector (optional)

L2 learners need to learn specific strategies for listening, including how to listen for content. Unlike the traditional reproduction exercise, in which students retell or summarize received information, the content word-deleted listening cloze requires reproduction only of the words that carry meaning.

Procedure

1. Select or write a passage and delete some content, or information, words (nouns, verbs, adjectives, and, in some cases, adverbs). The passage length and number of deletions are determined by the proficiency level:

Proficiency Level	Approximate Word Count	No. of Deletions
Beginning	50–65	8–12
Intermediate	75–90	14–16
Advanced	100–120	18–20

Note that the level of difficulty is lower than that of reading texts studied intensively at the targeted level. Sixty to seventy percent accuracy indicates the appropriate, challenging instructional level. Avoid using a passage that can be completed without *listening* (i.e., one in which the information is universally known).

2. Place the cloze passage face down on each student's desk. Permit no note-taking during listening. Explain the topic of the passage, if necessary.
3. Read the passage at normal speed two times.
4. Tell the students to turn the paper over and complete the passage by writing one word in each blank space. Allow about 10 minutes for completion.
5. Elicit answers from the students, writing all acceptable responses on the board or overhead projector. Self-checking and discussion provide valuable immediate feedback.

Caveats and Options

The content listening cloze is not graded by the word-exact method. If a word retains the meaning of the oral passage, it is correct. Keep in mind the context of the entire passage, as well as the sentence, to determine whether a substituted word is acceptable. Not surprisingly, the higher proficiency level of the students, the more substitutions they make. Because content is the focus, errors in tense and number, part of speech, and spelling are not counted wrong if the meaning is retained (see Appendix).

Appendix: Sample Content Listening Cloze

Level: Intermediate
Length: 94 words

An old story says that an Arabian (1) **merchant** made the first cheese. He put (2) **milk** in a pouch made from a sheep's (3) **stomach** before he (4) **traveled** across the desert. The movement of his (5) **camel**, the desert heat, and the (6) **chemicals** in the pouch made the milk (7) **separate**. The (8) **thick** part was the first cheese.

Today cheese is (9) **made** all over the world. Most if it is made from (10) **cow's** milk because the (11) **supply** of this milk is (12) **great**. Smaller (13) **amounts** are made from milk of other animals, such as (14) **sheep**, goats, and even (15) **reindeer**. (Words in bold are deleted in the cloze passage.)

Notes on grading: *Produced*, or even *found* may be substituted for (9) **made** and still retain the story's meaning. *Quantity* or *supplies* may be substituted for (13) **amounts**. *Traveler* or *man* may not be substituted for (1) **merchant** because these words do not retain the meaning, although *trader*, *peddlar*, or even *salesman* or *businessman* are acceptable.

Contributor

Gaye Childress is Curriculum Coordinator and Teacher Trainer for instruction in reading, listening, and speaking at the Intensive English Language Institute at the University of North Texas, Denton, in the United States.

Fred's Having a Party

Levels
Beginning

Aims
Develop the ability to
accurately comprehend
directions

Class Time
15–20 minutes

Preparation Time
20–25 minutes

Resources
Audiotape of someone
giving directions
Photocopies of a map

This exercise gives students the chance to rehearse real-life situations in which they have to rely on instructions to get to their destination.

Procedure

1. Give out maps to the students.
2. Check the students' readiness for the task by asking them to locate different points on the map, such as the railway stations and the bank.
3. Review such terms as *in front of, to the left, behind*, and so on by asking students to describe where places are on the map: "Where's the bank?" "It's next to the post office."
4. Tell the students that Fred is having a party and they have all been invited. Tell them that they are going to hear directions of how to get to Fred's house (which should be unmarked on the map) and that they have to draw the route from the railway station or other such location to Fred's house.
5. Play the tape as students listen to the tape and draw a line from the starting point to Fred's house.
6. Ask the students to check their directions with a partner. Optionally, do the activity again starting from a different point on the map.
7. As a follow-up exercise, have the students work in pairs using the lines that they have drawn to describe to each other how to get to Fred's house.

Caveats and Options

Provide a map that is only partially labeled. As an introductory exercise, ask students to write in, for example, where the, bank, the supermarket, or the hospital is. The tape could issue instructions such as "The restaurant is beside the flower shop" or "The theatre is opposite Harry's Nightclub."

Contributor

Dominic Cogan is a Lecturer in English at Fukui Prefectural University, Japan. He has also taught in Ireland, Ghana, Oman.

The Best Person for the Job

Levels
Intermediate +

Aims
Listen selectively for
specific information

Class Time
25–40 minutes

Preparation Time
30–40 minutes

Resources
Audiotape of candidates
being interviewed for a
job
Copies of a job
description and
candidate requirements

The activity is designed to encourage students to listen for specific points of information to solve a practical problem: the selection of the right person for the job.

Procedure

1. Give out a copy of the job description and requirements that you have drawn up. Check that the students understand the information.
2. Distribute a table similar to the following:

	Candidate 1	Candidate 2	Candidate 3
Age			
Years of experience			
Qualifications			
Job related skills			
Interests			

3. Play the tape of the three short interviews through. Ask students to fill in the Age and Years of experience rows as they listen.
4. Play the tape again but stop at the end of each interview to allow students to complete the table.
5. Play the whole tape through again so that students can check their work.
6. Divide the class into selection panels. Have members of each group check to see that they have similar data.
7. Ask each selection panel to choose the best candidate for the job by referring their data to the candidate requirements in the job description.

8. Have one student from each panel report to the whole class on their selection and the reasons for their choice of candidate.
9. Facilitate a whole-class discussion on the selection process.

Caveats and Options

Instead of writing the candidate requirements yourself, ask the students themselves to draw them up after being placed in their selection panel groups. Make the task more challenging by including a lot of superfluous information about each candidate on the tape.

Contributor

Dominic Cogan is a Lecturer in English at Fukui Prefectural University, Japan. He has also taught in Ireland, Ghana, Oman.

The Business Report

Levels
Intermediate

Aims
Develop the ability to listen for specific information

Class Time
10–15 minutes

Preparation Time
15–20 minutes

Resources
Audiotaped business report from the BBC World Service, CNN, or any local radio or TV station

This activity is especially useful for English for business studies students who have to get used to listening to currency movements. It is important to emphasize to the students that they are listening only for certain key words/phrases. They should realize that they will not understand many of the words used. However, this should not interfere with their ability to successfully complete the task.

Procedure

1. Elicit names of some of the major currencies in the world. Write these on the board (have students describe to you the symbol used for each currency or write the symbols on the board).
2. Elicit the countries to match the currencies that you have written on the board.
3. Ask the students to prepare a simple chart like the following on a sheet of paper and to write in the currencies that are on the board:

yen	złoty	lira	pound sterling
corona	mark		

4. Play the tape. Tell the students to tick the box if they hear the currency mentioned on the tape.
5. Tell the students to add to their table any other currencies which they heard mentioned on the tape. Play the tape a second time for the students to check their table.
6. Play the tape again. Tell the students to listen for the value of the currency and to write it on the table. Check the answers around the

class. (You may need to do some practice in saying numbers before this stage.)

7. Play the tape again. Tell the students to listen for words used to describe the currency, such as *fell* by, *dropped* by, *increased* by, *remained unchanged, reached a new high*. Tell the students to write down the word or phrase on the table. Check their answers and discuss the meaning of some of the words or phrases.

8. Using the information on the table, the students can now practice giving short business report to a partner.

9. As a follow-up activity, ask the students to listen to the evening business report on the radio and complete a similar chart. Check the information and use it for a discussion in the next lesson.

Contributor

Austin Conway is Language Instructor at the Hong Kong University of Science and Technology.

Meet the Teacher

Levels
Any

Aims
Get to know the teacher at the beginning of a new term/year
Practice taking notes from an interview
Practice the language of simple past, present perfect, future time, or idioms (depending on the interviewer and interviewee)

Class Time
15–30 minutes

Preparation Time
30 minutes

Procedure

1. Prepare a list of questions you want the interviewer to ask you about yourself. Have a friend or colleague interview you on tape (the more it sounds like a radio/TV talk show, the better. Of course, you will need to adjust your language to the level of your class). If you are going to do one of the variations below, prepare an appropriate handout.
2. On the first day of a new term/school year, tell your students that you were recently interviewed on a radio/TV talk show for famous teachers and that you have brought a copy of the interview on tape. They will have to note down as much information as possible.
3. Play the tape as many times as the students need to hear it.
4. In pairs or small groups, have the students discuss what they have heard and verify that they have the correct information.
5. Have each pair/small group share one thing they have learned about you and ask any additional questions they have.

Caveats and Options

1. Prepare an information table or a cloze, multiple choice, or true/false exercise for the students to fill out while they listen (depending on the level of the class).
2. As a follow-up activity, have the students interview each other and then report what they have learned to the rest of the class.
3. For homework, have students write a short biography of you, based on the interview.
4. For higher level classes, focus on idioms used in the interview.

Contributor

Mark Dickens teaches at Fields College International, Victoria, Canada.

Where Are the Scissors?

Levels
Beginning-low
intermediate

Aims
Identify the position of
an item based on
spoken language
Practice listening to
descriptions of the
position of an item
using the locators
*middle, left, right, top,
bottom*

Class Time
15–20 minutes

Preparation Time
None

Resources
Chalkboard, chalk

The basic language students need to do this activity includes location words (*middle, left, right, top, bottom*) and the terms *row* and *column*. Students often have a hard time with these last words. Students enjoy this activity because it is quick, student-generated, and offers useful, easy listening practice.

Procedure

1. Draw a large grid of three squares by three squares on the board. Across the top write *left, middle, right*. Along the left side, write *top, middle, bottom*. Write any nine letters of the alphabet in the boxes.
2. Explain the concept of row and column to the students. (This is not as easy as it might appear.) Practice extensively the position of the letters: The letter *J* is in the top row, the right column. The letter *B* is in the middle row, the left column. Students must have a good grasp of these terms before you go on to step two. For additional practice, have students write out the position of several letters. Have students work with a partner to tell where each letter is in the grid.
3. Draw nine simple objects on the board (e.g., a cat, a book, a pencil, the sun, a cloud, a house, a tree, a snake, scissors).
4. Demonstrate the activity with one student. You and the student each draw a grid (on paper or at different ends of the board if possible). One person begins by choosing any of the nine objects, drawing it anywhere in the grid, and then telling the partner where to draw that item. (The person whose name has the most letters in it goes first.) For example, the student chooses the cat, draws it in the top row, middle column, and then tells you, "Draw the cat in the top row, middle column." If you don't understand, ask for clarification "Excuse me. Could you please repeat that?" Choose any of the remaining

items, draw it in a square in the grid, and tell the student to draw the object in the corresponding square. Take turns until all nine squares on both players' papers have an object in them. At that point, compare papers. They should be *exactly the same*. (If there is a mistake, try to figure out how the mistake happened. Mistakes are as much a part of the learning process as the correct answers.)

5. Once the class has grasped the way this activity is done, have students work in pairs. Have each student draw a 3 x 3 grid and then have the partners take turns placing items and describing the position to their partner. To make sure students are actually communicating their information rather than just looking at their partner's papers, have students put folders or a similar object between themselves and their partner so that neither can see the other's paper.

Caveats and Options

You may want to increase the grid size to 4 x 4 (16 squares); however, it is better to play several smaller games than one large game because students will make errors, such as filling in the wrong square, because of miscommunication. In a short game, this miscommunication will not matter so much as you can easily begin again, but in a long game, it is often quite frustrating to the student who did not make the mistake, especially if the listening level of the two partners is unusually mismatched.

References and Further Reading

Folse, K. (1993). In the top row, right column. In K. Folse, *Talk a lot* (p. 78). Ann Arbor: University of Michigan Press.

Contributor

Keith S. Folse has taught English in the United States, Saudi Arabia, Malaysia, and Japan. He is the author of English Structure Practices, Intermediate Reading Practices, *and* Talk a Lot *(University of Michigan Press).*

Home Country Dictation

Levels
False beginning–
intermediate

Aims
Develop skill in
listening to specific
directions

Class Time
20 minutes

Preparation Time
30 minutes

Resources
Map of your home
country or state in two
versions: one in which
the names of major
cities, rivers, and so on
have been filled in, and
one in which they have
not
Information on the
various cities and other
landmarks in your home
country or state

This task-based activity focuses on understanding directions while providing students with some information about the teacher's home country or state. It is a good first-week activity.

Procedure

1. Pass out the maps of your home country or state without names. Be sure everyone has the map turned the correct way. Explain that this is your native country or state. Tell students that you are going to provide them with information about this area and that they should write in the names of cities, states, and other landmarks as you describe them.
2. Begin by describing the places that border your home country or state. As you say each place name, write it on the board so that the students can spell it correctly. For example, my home state is Washington in the United States, so I usually begin as follows:

   To the west of my state lies the Pacific Ocean.
   To the north lies Canada. Idaho is to the east, and
   Oregon is south of my state.

   I then usually ask if anyone can identify the name of my state.

3. Continue describing the location of cities, mountains, rivers, and other landmarks. After you describe the location of each place, give some facts about it. These could include average temperatures, annual snowfall or rainfall, main industries, population, distance between cities, or things to see and do.
4. Pass around or post a copy of the map that contains all the names so that the students can check their work.

Caveats and Options

This exercise will undoubtedly generate a number of questions about your home country or state. Either answer these as they arise or have a question-and-answer period after the exercise is complete.

Contributor

Kelly Fowler is Language Instructor at the Japan Intercultural Academy of Municipalities in Otsu City, Japan.

Listening to the Stock Market Report

Levels
Any

Aims
Practice listening to numbers

Class Time
20–30 minutes

Preparation Time
10 minutes

Resources
Audiotaped segment of a stock market report that gives about 20 prices

This exercise is particularly useful with business English classes but could be useful for any class that needs to practice listening to numbers.

Procedure

1. Preteach the sequence in which the information will occur, such as "Rex Crude Oil up 23 at 156.8."
2. Give each student a worksheet containing the relevant company names (see Appendix for a template for creating worksheets).
3. Instruct the students to listen and write in the numbers they hear. Play the tape through without stopping.
4. Ask the students to compare their answers with a partner.
5. Play the tape again to allow the students to check their answers.
6. Ask individual students to read out their answers while the rest of the class listens and checks their work. (It may be necessary to do some practice in saying the numbers before this stage.)

(continued)

**Appendix:
Template for
Worksheets**

Name of Company	Up/Down	How Much?	Price Now
EXAMPLE: Trent Oil	Up/Down	0.23	US$18.6
	Up/Down		
	Up/Down		
	Up/Down		
	Up/Down		
	Up/Down		
	Up/Down		
	Up/Down		
	Up/Down		
	Up/Down		

Contributor

David Gardner teaches English for special purposes in the English Centre of the University of Hong Kong. He has taught in secondary, technical, and tertiary institutions in a number of countries.

Make Questions—Task 1

Levels
Low intermediate

Aims
Listen for specific information

Class Time
15–20 minutes

Preparation Time
20 minutes

Resources
Short, factual audio- or videotape (e.g., an item from a news broadcast, a weather report, a section of a documentary, or a public service announcement)

Listening in order to construct questions is more demanding than listening for answers. It requires the listener to gather more information, and the resulting production must be more complete.

Procedure

1. Prepare short-form answers for five questions that can be answered by listening to the recording.
2. Write on the board several short-form answers related to the listening activity.
3. Tell the students that they must produce questions for the answers on the board.
4. Play the recording once.
5. Allow the students some time to write their questions.
6. Play the recording a second time to allow the students to check their questions and make adjustments if required.
7. Ask individual students to call out a question and identify the answer from the board.

Caveats and Options

Impose restrictions on question content, such as geographical, political, or historical. Or control the question format through the answers chosen, example, to practice *wh*-questions, answers should include times, places, people, and so on. To practice other kinds of questions, answers should be Yes or No with optional extras, such as *No, not today.*

Contributor

David Gardner teaches ESP in the English Centre of the University of Hong Kong. He has taught in secondary, technical, and tertiary institutions in a number of countries.

Make Questions—Task 2

Levels
Intermediate

Aims
Speculate

Class Time
15–20 minutes

Preparation Time
20 minutes

Resources
A short audio or video recording of factual nature (such as an item from a news broadcast, weather report, section of documentary, public service announcement)

To construct questions on the basis of the speculative answers given, students are required to understand the degree of probability in the original statement.

Procedure

1. Prepare short-form answers for five questions that can be answered by listening to the recording. All answers should indicate degrees of possibility/probability, such as *It's quite possible, That seems very unlikely, Definitely not, It may happen.*
2. Write on the board the short-form answers to questions that can be asked concerning the listening exercise.
3. Inform the students that they must produce questions for the answers on the board.
4. Play the recording once, then give the students some time to write their questions.
5. Play the recording a second time so that the students can check their questions and make adjustments if required.
6. Ask individual students to call out a question that corresponds to an answer on the board.

Contributor

David Gardner teaches ESP in the English Centre of the University of Hong Kong. He has taught in secondary, technical, and tertiary institutions in a number of countries.

Make Questions—Task 3

Levels
High intermediate

Aims
Listen for specific
information

Class Time
10–15 minutes

Preparation Time
15 minutes

Resources
A radio or TV broadcast
of a factual nature to
which all students have
access (a news
broadcast, weather
report, or documentary)

Working on a live broadcast is much more demanding than using recorded material. It is important that all students listen to the same broadcast (and that the teacher does too) so that they can support each other during feedback.

Procedure

1. Prepare a generic worksheet containing 20 short-form answers (or use the one in the Appendix). The answers must be sufficiently general to suit a variety of broadcasts. The bonus is that the same worksheet can be used for different exercises.
2. Give out the worksheet to the students near the end of the class.
3. Tell the students that they must produce questions for any five of the answers given on the worksheet for homework.
4. Decide with the class which broadcast they will listen to.
5. At the next lesson arrange the students into small groups and ask them to discuss the questions they wrote.
6. If possible, bring the broadcast the students listened to into the class and allow them to listen to it again after their discussion. Discuss with the class the most suitable questions for the answers on the worksheet.

Caveats and Options

In cases where students do not have access to such broadcasts, make a recording available in a library or for home use.

Appendix: Sample Worksheet

No.	Answer	No.	Answer
1	Without doubt.	11	Probably.
2	The outcome is uncertain.	12	Sometime in the future.
3	It's impossible to predict.	13	It's a question of politics.
4	Yesterday.	14	It's a question of money.
5	It's finished.	15	That's unlikely to happen.
6	It's continuing.	16	It's being negotiated.
7	Not good.	17	Making an official visit.
8	Bad.	18	It's a dangerous place to be at the moment.
9	Disastrous.	19	There seems to be a lot of activity there.
10	Maybe.	20	It's possible.

Your Questions:

(Please indicate the answer number)

1. _____
   _____

2. _____
   _____

3. _____
   _____

4. _____

_____

5. _____

_____

Contributor

David Gardner teaches ESP in the English Centre of the University of Hong Kong. He has taught in secondary, technical, and tertiary institutions in a number of countries.

Math Challenge

Levels
Beginning–low
intermediate

Aims
Practice listening for
and processing numbers

Class Time
10 minutes

Preparation Time
5–10 minutes

Resources
List of math problems
Keyboard (or tape of
one- and two-octave
scales)

Although most students learn numbers soon after starting to study English, most have difficulty actually using them when they are presented out of sequence, as is usual outside the classroom.

Procedure

1. Before class, write out 10-12 math problems and calculate the answers. They should be at a level that learners will find challenging but possible to solve in 8-10 seconds.
2. Bring a keyboard or xylophone to class. If it isn't practical to have one in the classroom, record a scale at the rate of about one note per second. You may want to record the scale several times so you don't have to rewind the tape.
3. Begin by preteaching the math function vocabulary the students will need (*plus, minus, times, divided by*).
4. Tell the students that they will hear some math problems. They have to write them and find the answer as fast as they can. They should raise their hands as soon as they find the answer.
5. Read out the first problem twice. As soon as you have finished saying it the second time, start to play a one-octave musical scale on the keyboard or xylophone. Learners try to solve the problem before the scale is finished.
6. When you've finished the scale, have learners call out the answer. Write it on the board.
7. Continue with the rest of the problems.

Caveats and Options

1. If you want to do more difficult math problems, record or play a two-octave scale to give students more time to work. Math can be boring

for many students (and teachers). However, adding the musical scale adds interest because it allows the learners to compete against themselves to find the answer before the scale is finished.

2. Even at lower levels, it is unlikely that simple math problems will take anywhere near 8 seconds to solve. Students almost instantly know the answers once they understand the problems. In that case, consider giving the students the answer, then reading two math problems. Learners have to figure out which math problem will give them the answer.

Example:

The problems: 63 + 44 or 46 + 51
The answer is 107

Contributors

Marc Helgesen is Associate Professor at Miyagi Gakuin Women's College, Sendai, Japan. Steven Brown is Curriculum Coordinator at the University of Pittsburgh English Language Institute in the United States. They are coauthors of the Active Listening series (Cambridge University Press) and the New English Firsthand series (Longman/Lingual House).

Family Photo

Levels
Low intermediate

Aims
Listen for specific information in order to describe and identify people accurately

Class Time
10–15 minutes

Preparation Time
15–20 minutes

Resources
Photograph of an extended family, such as a wedding photo or a family reunion photo Audiotape of grandmother and granddaughter talking about members of the family in the photograph

Students, both as speakers and listeners, need to be accurate in their descriptions of people so as to avoid confusion and embarrassment.

Procedure

1. Describe someone in the classroom very generally, such as "This person has black hair, wears glasses and is learning English." Elicit guesses as to who is being described. Be as vague as to make it virtually impossible to guess accurately. Use this experience to illustrate the need for specific and accurate descriptions.
2. Distribute a copy of the family photo to each student.
3. Have students scrutinize the photo and try to identify the different generations individually and silently.
4. Play the tape while students listen to the descriptions and write the names of the people being described in the photograph.
5. Elicit the names from the students.
6. Ask the students to prepare a table (see below).
7. Play the tape again. Have students complete the table by supplying names, ages, and main features. For example:

Name	Age	Main Features
Uncle John	78	Long beard, no hair, toothless
_____	____	_____

8. Play the tape again so that students can check their answers.
9. As a class activity, ask the students to use their tables to describe the people in the photograph. If there is any disagreement, play the tape again and stop it at the relevant information.

Caveats and Options

Give the students a cut-up photo of an extended family (each person is cut out separately). While listening to the tape describing the people and their position, the students arrange the cut out people to reconstruct the photo.

Contributor

Geraldine Hetherton is currently working as an ESOL teacher in Japan. She has also taught ESOL in Ireland, Ghana, and Oman.

What's in the News?

Levels
Intermediate

Aims
Extract specific
information from a
stream of talk and
organize that
information

Class Time
20–30 minutes

Preparation Time
15 minutes

Resources
Audiotape of the
headlines of a news
broadcast
Chalkboard or overhead
projector

Extracting specific information from a large body of words is an important skill. Students in particular need to develop the ability to organize such information so that it is clear, understandable, and easily retrieved. This task will enhance their note-taking skills.

Procedure

1. Have a brief open discussion in which you elicit the main current news items from the students.
2. Ask the students what they think will be in the news today.
3. Distribute a worksheet with a table of possible news topics and a grid (see Appendix).
4. Have the students scan the worksheet and raise any problems/uncertainties they might have.
5. Have the students listen to the tape and number the news topics in order of occurrence. Remind the students that not all the topics will be covered.
6. Elicit answers to the following questions:

   How many news topics did you hear?
   Which was first (second, and so on)?

7. Replay the tape and ask the students to complete the following:

   What   When   Where   Extra Information
   _____   _____   _____   _____

8. Replay the tape as the students check the information.
9. Elicit the information from the students and complete the grid on the chalkboard or overhead projector.

Caveats and Options

1. Play the first news item again while the students note the adjectives used. Discuss the effect the use of such adjectives have on the particular news item and on the listener.
2. Depending on time, explore other news items likewise.
3. Explore verbs used in a similar manner.

Appendix: Sample Worksheet

Topic	Order
Business and Finance	
The Arts/Entertainment	
Domestic politics	1
Crime	
International Politics	
Weather	
Disasters/Accidents	
Sports	

Contributor

Geraldine Hetherton is currently working as an ESOL teacher in Japan. She has also taught ESOL in Ireland, Ghana, and Oman.

What Do I Do (About the Simple Present)?

Levels
Beginning

Aims
Practice adverbs of
frequency and the
simple present

Class Time
15 minutes

Preparation Time
5 minutes

Resources
Chalkboard
Paper and pencils

This activity helps students to distinguish between adverbs of frequency (e.g., *sometimes, rarely*) and reinforces the use of the simple present to describe habits and routines.

Procedure

1. Elicit the adverbs from students and have students copy them down in a row, ranging from *never* to *always*:

   never   seldom   sometimes   often   usually   always

2. Explain to the class that you will dictate to them about your habits/ routines. Their task is to listen and write a word/phrase under the appropriate heading. For example

   I go shopping three times a week.
   I can't swim, so I don't go to the swimming pool.
   I call my parents every night.

never	seldom	sometimes	often	usually	always
swim				shopping	call parents

3. Check as you would check other dictations.

Caveats and Options

1. Develop this idea further by letting students continue in pairs. First they compose sentences about their routines and then guess their partner's. This is a good time to check their production of the simple present.
2. This column dictation was inspired by Davis and Rinvolucri's (1988) *Dictation*.

References and Further Reading

Davis, P., & Rinvolucri, M. (1988). *Dictation: New methods, new possibilities*. Cambridge: Cambridge University Press.

Contributor

Van Le is Language Instructor at the Japan Intercultural Academy of Municipalities. She has edited Hands on Team Teaching (Hokkaido AJET), *a collection of simple teaching for language teaching ideas in Japanese. Her interests include English as an international language, computer-assisted instruction, and intercultural education.*

Picasso Dictation

Levels
Any

Aims
Practice listening to
descriptions of places,
spacial relations, and
prepositions of place

Class Time
10–15 minutes

Preparation Time
5 minutes

Resources
Paper and pencils
Description of a place
(either audiotaped or
read aloud by the
teacher in the class)

Unlike most dictations, which focus students' attention on individual words, this activity focuses students' attention on meaning and asks them to express that meaning in graphic form.

Procedure

1. Tell students to listen to a description of a place and to draw a picture based on what they hear.
2. Describe the place, sentence by sentence. An appropriate description for low intermediate students might be as follows:

   I have a small but comfortable living room. In the middle of the room is a coffee table, surrounded by four large cushions which I use to sit on. I don't have a sofa or any armchairs, but I have a long bookshelf on the western wall where I keep lots of novels, my stereo, and my CD collection. I love plants and have eight large plants along the southern wall so that they can catch the maximum sunlight from my picture window.

3. Have the students draw the scene as you read the description.
4. After completing the task, have students in pairs or groups compare and discuss their drawings before listening to the description once more.

Caveats and Options

1. Adapt this activity for different levels of students by varying the level of sophistication of the description.
2. Have students work in pairs to give each other the dictation. Give one student a picture to describe as the other student draws the picture.

Contributor

Charles Lockhart is University Lecturer, the City University of Hong Kong. He is coauthor of Reflective Teaching in Second Language Classrooms *(Cambridge University Press).*

Blind Drawing

Levels
High beginning

Aims
Practice listening to
prepositions and names
of objects

Class Time
10 minutes

Preparation Time
10 minutes

Resources
Four or five simple
drawings of situations,
such as a room, the
outside of a house, or
an office
Chalkboard, chalk

This is a variation on the describe-and-draw activity. The added interest here is that the illustrators have their eyes covered so must listen carefully to the information and try to imagine the picture.

Procedure

1. As a warm-up activity, describe a simple picture to the students while they draw what they hear. Have them compare their drawings.
2. Ask for two or three volunteers (depending on the size of the chalkboard).
3. Tell the volunteers to come to the front of the class and face the board. Then blindfold the students.
4. Tell the students facing the board to listen to the description and try to draw what they hear on the board. (If you feel brave enough, let the rest of the class shout out instructions to the drawers: *more to the left, more to the right, up a bit, down a bit,* etc.)
5. After you have finished giving the description tell the illustrators to take their blindfolds off. Vote for the "best" drawing, or ask students what problems there are in the drawings: "You said *above* the door, and she drew it *on* the door."

Contributor

Lindsay Miller is a Lecturer in the English Department at the City University of Hong Kong. He has taught EFL in Europe, the Middle East, and Southeast Asia.

What's in a Face?

Levels
Intermediate +

Aims
Discuss character and
personality
Practice using
speculative language
(e.g., *It could be . . .*, *He
might have a . . .*)

Class Time
20–30 minutes

Preparation Time
Varies

Resources
Six to eight photographs
of staff members,
photocopied onto a
handout

A lot of communication is affected by how much we like a person at first sight. We judge people (correctly or otherwise) by their appearance. Finding out more about people may change our initial perspective on them. The following activity is best done at the beginning of the year or with a new class before they get to know any of the staff members.

Procedure

1. Audiotape staff members talking about themselves. The staff should first introduce themselves: "I'm John. I'm 37 and single. I have black hair with a few gray hairs showing at the side. I like outdoor activities like swimming, wind surfing and hiking." Then, have two or three staff members cover personal topics: family, hobbies, where they have worked, and so on.
2. Engage the class in a warm-up discussion about how people are attracted to each other. Find out what sort of people various members of the class like meeting and talking to.
3. Arrange the students into groups of three or four. Distribute the photocopy of the staff members' photographs.
4. Tell the students to look at the photographs and, in their groups, discuss what kind of person they think the people in the photos are (you may want to preteach some vocabulary before this stage).
5. Tell the students that they will first hear the speaker introduce himself/herself. Have the students listen to the tape, try to identify who is speaking, and write the name under the photo.
6. Check the names with the photos to make sure everyone has the same answer.
7. Tell the students that they are going to hear the speakers talking about their lives. Play the tape once only. As they listen they should try to

identify who is talking and write some notes around the photograph (e.g., Bob, loves cooking, worked Iran, married, 5 kids, motor cars).
8. In their groups, have students compare the information about the people on the tape.

Caveats and Options

Follow up by having students write about the person they liked most from the tape or hold a group discussion about the student's character, personality, and lifestyle.

Contributor

Lindsay Miller is a Lecturer in the English Department at the City University of Hong Kong. He has taught EFL in Europe, the Middle East, and Southeast Asia.

Describe My Room

Levels
Any

Aims
Practice listening for information
Practice positional words and object descriptions

Class Time
1 hour

Preparation Time
10–15 minutes

Resources
Written description and picture of a room (or whatever is being described)
Paper for drawing

This activity shows how to teach effective listening with little or no technology. It also shows how listening can be integrated into other parts of a lesson.

Procedure

1. Tell the students that they are going to hear a description of a room. Read the description and ask them what you described.
2. Ask the students to draw a chart on a piece of paper with the following headings:

Position	Object	Description

3. Read the description again. Have students fill in as much information as they can on their chart.
4. Have the students work in pairs. They do not show each other their charts but use the information in the chart to talk about the room. Students who have missed some information can now try to complete the chart.
5. Have the students either draw a picture of the room using the information in the chart or write a description of the room. Show the students the picture of the room and describe it once more.

Contributor

Gary Motteram is a Lecturer in Education in the teaching of English Overseas and Course Coordinator for the MEd in Educational Technology and TESOL at Manchester University, England.

What's the Weather Like?

Levels
Low intermediate

Aims
Practice listening for
specific information

Class Time
15 minutes

Preparation Time
15–20 minutes

Resources
Audiotaped weather
forecast from radio or
TV for five or six cities

It is important to teach students that listening can be successful even though they do not understand every single word of an aural text.

Procedure

1. Remind students that listening can be successful without understanding every word.
2. Play the weather forecasts. Have students call out when they hear the name of a city.
3. Pause the tape and write the cities on board.
4. Create a chart around the cities like the following:

City	Today		Tomorrow	
	High	Low	High	Low

5. Play the tape again as students call out the high and low temperatures for each city. Fill in the chart.

60

6. Put the following list on the chalkboard (items on the list may vary, depending on the nature of the forecasts):

Item   City
Umbrella
Sweater
Suntan lotion
Sunglasses
Hat

7. Ask students where it would be useful to have these things. Play the tape one more time and elicit responses from the students.

Caveats and Options

Add a Key Words heading to the list on the chalkboard. Play the tape again, and have students nominate key weather words. Write these in against the appropriate cities.

Contributor

David Nunan is Professor of Applied Linguistics and Director of the English Centre at the University of Hong Kong. He is the author of Atlas: A Course in Learning Centered Communication *(Heinle & Heinle).*

Swapping Houses

Levels
Intermediate

Aims
Develop skill in
listening for the gist as
well as specific
information
Develop intensive
listening skill

Class Time
45 minutes

Preparation Time
20 minutes +

Resources
Several taped
conversation extracts on
the topic of swapping
houses for the summer

A worksheet similar to the examples shown below. Students often have difficulty listening to a speaker on the telephone. Features of real speech, such as interruption, hesitations, pauses, and unclear speech should all form part of the taped dialogues so as to give students practice in this real-life activity. Note that some students may not be familiar with the concept of swapping houses for vacation, so the teacher may have to explain this first.

Procedure

1. As a warm-up activity, ask the students to draw the house of their dreams. Elicit some useful vocabulary from the students about houses by asking them to describe their houses.
2. Tell the students that they are going to hear four telephone conversation extracts of different people who are in the process of negotiating a house exchange.
3. Give the students a table similar to the following:

Next to each statement write the number of the extract you think it relates to (two of the statements cannot be matched)

Statement   Extract No.

a. There are some sports facilities.
b. It is suitable for people who suffer from headaches.
c. There is an airport nearby.
d. There are two children in the family.
e. Pets are not allowed.
f. There is a lift in the building.

After the students have read through the statements, play the conversation extracts and ask them to write down the number of the extract opposite the statement. Then check the answers with the class.

4. Tell the students that they are now going to listen for specific information. Focus their attention on the second worksheet task:

For each dialogue that you hear, tick one box only:

Dialogue 1
Underground station nearby ☐
Bus service only ☐
No transport facilities ☐

Dialogue 2
Restaurants in neighborhood ☐
Noisy street ☐
Good shopping facilities ☐

Dialogue 3
Children like swimming ☐
Husband is a good cook ☐
Family owns a dog ☐

Dialogue 4
There is a park nearby ☐
Sports center is far away ☐
Eldest son likes swimming ☐

Play the dialogues a second time and ask the students to complete the second worksheet. Check the answers with the class.

5. Finally, focus the students' attention on a more complex intensive listening task.

Listen carefully and decide which item(s) are mentioned in each conversation. Tick them:

	House	Apartment	Buses	Underground	Sports Fac.	Peaceful	Shops	Children	Park
Extract 1									
Extract 2									
Extract 3									
Extract 4									

After playing the tape a third time, ask the students to check their answers in groups.

6. As a follow-up activity, ask the students to discuss which house they would like to spend their vacation in and why.

Contributors

Pilar Perez Freire and Emeterio Guitian Quiroga are secondary school teachers of English in Spain.

Sssnakes

Levels
Any

Aims
Practice *s* for third person, plurals, and possessives

Class Time
20 minutes

Preparation Time
30 minutes

Resources
Specially prepared text with many examples of *s* endings, some missing

Students often have problems with what seem to them to be unimportant aspects of grammar. This exercise helps focus their attention on such a case.

Procedure

1. Arrange the students into A and B pairs. Give all the As a copy of the text. Tell the students that only the As are allowed to see the text to begin with.
2. Tell the As to read the text to the Bs. The Bs sit and listen.
3. Tell the As to read the text again to the Bs. This time the Bs must listen for *s* endings. If they do not hear an *s* but think that there should be one in the word, they must stop the reader by saying "snakes." Student A should then insert an *s* onto the end of the word that he last said (if B was late in saying *snakes,* A should insert the *s* on the last word she said).
4. Once A has read the story twice and inserted as many *s* as B identifies, have A give the text to B, who then reads the text out loud while A listens to the story and says *snakes* whenever she does not hear an *s*, or when she hear an *s* where there should not be one.
5. After all students have completed the task, read out the text while the students listen and read their altered texts.

Contributor

Elizabeth A. Price is an ESOL teacher with the British Council.

Advertising

Levels
Low intermediate

Aims
Develop skill in
listening for gist and
specific information
Become aware of how
language creates an
effect
Develop ability to use
visual clues when
listening

Class Time
30 minutes

Preparation Time
15–20 minutes

Resources
Several videotaped TV
advertisements

Visual clues can aid listening comprehension and develop students' ability to use the context to understand what is being said.

Procedure

1. Discuss advertising on TV generally. Ask what the students' favorite-least favorite advertisements are and why. Discuss devices used in advertising, such as slogans, jingles, and logos.
2. Preteach any vocabulary you feel may be problematic (this is optional, as you may wish students to guess the meaning of all the words in the advertisement).
3. Play the tape. Ask students to make a note of the most important words and phrases they hear in the advertisements. Ask the students to fill in a chart similar to the one below:

Ad	Language
1.	
2.	
3.	

4. Play the tape three or four times and pause it after each advertisement to give the students time to complete their notes.
5. Ask the class for any language they heard and make a note of the answers on the board. Replay the tape for clarification if necessary. Encourage students to guess the meaning of words/phrases they are not sure of and to guess what was said if they are not sure.
6. Discuss the advertisements with the class. Focus on how much they could understand without visual clues. Play the advertisements again and get the students to describe what they think the visuals are like.

Try to get the students to describe any advertisements they know of that used only visuals and no language.

Caveats and Options

1. Elicit vocabulary first and use it as the key words from which phrases could be built. Focus on the use of comparatives/superlatives and/or the use of adjectives in general.
2. Choose one product type and have the students compare the language used (e.g., cars, washing powder). If a video is impractical, use the radio.

Contributor

Jackie Wheeler is Language Instructor at the Hong Kong University of Science and Technology.

What's On?

Levels
Intermediate

Aims
Practice listening for
specific information

Class Time
20–25 minutes

Preparation Time
15–20 minutes

Resources
Audiotaped tourist
board announcement of
what there is to do in a
city the students are
familiar with, including
names of places, times
of opening and closing,
cost of admissions
Map of the same city

This activity reminds students that it is not always necessary to understand every word in order to listen successfully.

Procedure

1. Elicit suggestions from the students about the major tourist sights of the city and write them on the board. Ask the students the kind of important information it is necessary to know about such places, such as time of opening, cost, and bus route. From the information you receive from the students, create a chart on the board similar to the one below:

	Opening Time	Closing Time	Cost of Admission	Bus No.
Buckingham Palace				
The Tower				
Madame Tussaud's				
The British Museum				

2. Ask the students to copy the chart.
3. Play the tape and tell the students to listen for any places mentioned that are on their table. Tick the places mentioned. Add other places mentioned on the tape but not on the chart.
4. Play the tape a second time and ask the students to complete the information on the chart.
5. Give the students a map of the city and a budget (this can be different for each student) and ask them to plan a day's sightseeing, taking into account opening times, cost, and other factors.

6. Have the students work in groups explaining their day's sightseeing.

Caveats and Options

Give the students the same budget and have them work together to plan a day's sightseeing. This type of group activity is useful for practicing negotiation, persuading, agreeing, and disagreeing.

Contributor

Julie Wilkinson teaches at the British Council, Bangkok, and has several years' experience teaching in England, France, and Greece.

◆ Predicting
How Shall I Say It?

Levels
High intermediate +

Aims
Cope with problems of
translating ideas from
their L1 to the target
language

Class Time
25–30 minutes

Preparation Time
15 minutes

Resources
Short videotaped TV
programs with
dialogues in English and
subtitles in the students'
L1

These activities give students instant feedback on listening-translation practice. The exercises will give them opportunities to translate subtitles into English and to access the accuracy of their comprehension by listening to the actual speech.

Procedure

1. Explain to the class what the videotape is about (optional).
2. Play a short segment of the videotape minus the sound. Ask the students to watch the screen and to read the foreign language subtitles.
3. Ask the students to write an English translation of the subtitles (a time limit can be placed on this activity).
4. Play the tape again minus the sound.
5. Pair students up and ask them to read what they have written and agree on one translation.
6. Play the tape again, but with the sound.
7. Have students work in their pairs again and read over their translations.
8. Discuss with the students any problems they had in writing the translation.
9. Play the tape again stopping when students want to raise a question about their translation. Discuss acceptable alternatives.

Caveats and Options

Have students work individually, in pairs or in groups for the above activity.

Contributor

Erlinda R. Boyle is Senior Instructor at the English Language Teaching Unit of the Chinese University of Hong Kong.

Predictions

Levels
Intermediate

Aims
Listen intensively for
detailed information

Class Time
30 minutes

Preparation Time
20 minutes

Resources
Video cassette recorder
(VCR)
Short video
documentary extract
(e.g. Television English,
Video Report, Central
News or television
broadcasts, where
copyright permits)

This activity helps students learn that they don't have to understand every word to understand the topic of a passage.

Procedure

1. Identify in advance (using the VCR counter) brief segments that give clues to the topic without being too explicit.
2. Inform the class that they are going to see a brief segment of a documentary and that they should note down the key points while they watch.
3. Play the first 2 minutes of the segment of the video.
4. Ask the students to predict the topic by using their notes and to discuss what they think will follow on the tape.
5. Play the whole extract of the video and allow the students to check their predictions.
6. Ask the students to identify any relevant language clues that helped them make their predictions.

References and Further Reading

Television English is published by BBC English.
Video Report is available from The Language Centre, Brighton University.
Central News is published by Oxford University Press.

Contributor

David Gardner teaches English for special purposes in the English Centre of the University of Hong Kong. He has taught in secondary, technical, and tertiary institutions in a number of countries.

Culture Cards

Levels
Beginning +

Aims
Use schema to help
guessing
Practice making
descriptions and work
on the distinction
between plural and
singular pronouns and
verb agreement
Develop subtlety in
the L2

Class Time
20–40 minutes

Preparation Time
10–30 minutes initially

Resources
Several small cards with
students' L1 culture
words
Blank cards for students
to write their own

Playing a guessing game based on students' own culture takes advantage of schema (Ur, 1984) to help students guess from what they are able to hear, thus raising their confidence in their listening ability.

Procedure

1. Before class, make a starter set of culture cards. On each card, write a word or words that designate one thing from the culture (e.g., *uchiwa*, which is a Japanese fan). (If you live in the students' country, you may know enough about the culture to make a set of cards on your own. You can also get a colleague, or some students from that country, to help you make a starter set.)

2. Deal out the culture cards, face down, onto a desk at the front of the classroom. Divide the class into teams, and explain that in this game they will describe things, people, places, and so forth. from their country. The first team to guess what it is gets a point. Also explain that there can be only one guess per hint.

3. Pick a card, then give hints until someone guesses the item correctly. Subtle hints make the guessing more difficult. For example, to describe a Japanese *uchiwa*:

Hints
1. This is something that is often colorful.
2. It's made of wood and paper.
3. It opens and closes.
4. You can hold it in your hand.
5. It is sometimes used in classical dance.
6. It makes a breeze. . . .

4. After someone guesses correctly, give that person's team a point, draw another card, and give hints to describe it.
5. After you have done the first four or five cards, have students come up and give hints. Help any student who seems stuck. (Note: To discourage students from giving hints that are too direct—for *uchiwa* to say "This is a Japanese paper fan"—you may want to subtract points from a team if the person describes the thing too directly.)
6. Continue until every student has had a turn to draw a card and give hints, until all the cards have been drawn, or until the designated time is up. Tally the points and declare a winner.
7. Have students write more cards, if you wish, to be able to play again at a future date and to expand your set for other classes.

Caveats and Options

You may be able to use this game in an ESOL setting if the class contains enough of any one L1 learners to have at least one per team. In this case, after someone guesses what's on a card, the learners with the relevant L1 can expand about what it is and how the item is a part of their culture.

References and Further Reading

Ur, P. (1984). *Teaching listening comprehension.* Cambridge: Cambridge University Press.

Contributor

Kenny Harsch, Director of English Education at Kobe YMCA College, Japan, is interested in learner autonomy, student-centered curriculum development, and helping students develop curiosity through inquiry.

I Think I Know What She's Going to Say N. . . .

Levels
Intermediate +

Aims
Develop the strategy of
predicting what will be
heard in conversations

Class Time
20–25 minutes

Preparation Time
Varies

Resources
Taped conversation

One way of fostering active listening in your students is to give them practice in listening with the purpose of predicting what they will hear next.

Procedure

1. Before class, decide where you can stop the taped conversation; choose places where your students have a fair chance of guessing what a speaker will say next. (If possible, use a transcript to do this.) (See Appendix.)
2. In class, play the tape, stopping at the places you have chosen.
3. Have your students explain with reasons what they expect the speaker to say next.
4. Play the next part of the tape. If necessary, pause again and discuss any differences between what the students expected to hear and what was actually said.

References and Further Reading

Ur, P. (1987). *Teaching listening comprehension*. Cambridge: Cambridge University Press.

Appendix: Sample Conversation

Asterisks (*) show where you could stop the tape to elicit from your students what they expect to hear next.

A: How was the new restaurant, Bella?
B: I rather liked it. They have very good homemade soups. I had French onion soup, and it was * delicious. But their main courses * aren't quite as good.

A: Oh really? what didn't you like about them?
B: Well, although the meat dishes are OK, the vegetables * are awful— I mean they're overcooked and absolutely tasteless. I had carrots and potatoes, and I had to leave all my carrots, and I only * ate some of my potatoes. I nearly said something to the waiter.

A: But why didn't * you complain? If no one ever complains, they won't realize customers are dissatisfied, and they'll go on cooking vegetables in the same way.
B: Well, the service was very good, and the waiter was * nice and helpful. My husband's a vegetarian, so he couldn't * have any of the meat dishes on the menu. But the waiter went and asked the chef * to cook something special for him.

A: That was nice of him. And what are their desserts like?
B: Actually, both my husband and I are trying to lose weight, so * we didn't have any desserts. But they looked good.

A: You know, I think I'll go there myself. But I'm not a nice person like you. If the vegetables are * bad, I'll definitely complain.

Contributor

Jonathan Hull is a doctoral candidate at the University of Bristol, England. He has taught ESOL in Europe, the Mideast, East Asia, and the Pacific. He is a coauthor (under Jack C. Richards) of Interchange *(Cambridge University Press).*

What Comes Next?

Levels
Intermediate

Aims
Practice prediction
listening using stressed
words

Class Time
15 minutes

Preparation Time
30 minutes

Resources
Multiple choice handout
Teacher's list of
utterances (may be
taped)

It's useful for students to understand how to use prediction to improve their listening. Prediction at the microlevel is a bottom-up process in which incoming sounds are used to predict what comes next. This activity shows students how they can use word stress to help them predict an utterance that follows.

Procedure

1. Compile a list of utterances for which meaning is influenced by stress.
2. Prepare a handout of multiple-choice extensions for each utterance. The first part of the utterance should not appear on the handouts, and the extensions should be short and easy to read by the students.

   John wasn't late YESTERDAY. . .
   1. a. Sarah was.
      b. He was late today.
      c. He was early.

The first question should be an example, showing the correct choice for the second part of the utterance circled, as above.

3. Explain to the students that it is sometimes possible to predict what comes after an utterance if they listen to the stress. Give them one example.
4. Give the students time to read each of the choices for the first utterance. Read the utterance and allow about 10 seconds for the students to make a choice.
5. Provide immediate feedback by reading the correct answer. Repeat Steps 4 and 5 for each utterance.

Caveats and Options

1. Have the students simply guess to themselves what type of utterance will come next. This variation can precede the activity above. Be sure to provide immediate feedback so that the students can see if their predictions match.
2. Have the students write out their predictions.

Contributor

Jeff Johnson teaches English at Nova Intercultural Institute in Yokohama, Japan.

Paired Storytelling

Levels
Intermediate +

Aims
Develop an appropriate
purpose for listening
Build on prior
knowledge

Class Time
50 minutes

Preparation Time
15–20 minutes

Resources
Audiotaped narrative
texts or dialogues

Providing a purpose and activating the appropriate cultural schemata motivates students to listen to foreign messages and to maximize comprehension.

Procedure

1. Pair off students.
2. Provide a general introduction to the topic.
3. Divide the taped story or dialogue into two segments. Give the first half to one student in each pair and the second half to the other one. They will then listen to their own story segments without taking any notes.
4. Have the students listen to the same segments for the second time and jot down the key concepts found in the sections. Each student is to list the key words/phrases in the order in which they appear in the text.
5. Have the students in the pair exchange their lists. Give them a few moments to reflect on the list of clues and relate them to the story part they have heard.
6. Have each student develop and write his own version of the story's missing part. The student who has listened to the first half tries to predict what will happen next by recalling the part she has listened to, using the clues about the other part, and continuing to develop the story. The one who has listened to the latter part guesses what has happened before.
7. When they have finished, have the students read their own versions to each other.
8. Let everybody listen to the other tape segment and ask them to compare it with their own stories.

9. Conclude with a discussion of the whole story. Either in pairs or with the whole class.

Caveats and Options

Ask a few volunteers to read their stories aloud to the class.

Contributor

Anita Lie is a Lecturer in the English Department, Petra Christian University, Indonesia. She is currently completing her doctoral program in the School of Education, Baylor University, in the United States.

Guessing the Gaps

Levels
Beginning–intermediate

Aims
Listen to and
comprehend dialogues

Class Time
20 minutes

Preparation Time
10 minutes

Resources
Worksheets containing
cloze dialogues
Audiotape of scripted
dialogue

Many course books and listening skills textbooks have scripted dialogues with accompanying audiotapes. The following activity offers teachers a fresh way of exploiting these dialogues so that the students will be motivated to listen attentively and creatively.

Procedure

1. Reproduce a copy of a dialogue from a course book or listening skills book you are using with your class. Omit the lines of one of the interlocutors, as shown below:

   Sam: When do you think you'll be back?
   Yoko: _____
   Sam: As late as that. Where are you going?
   Yoko: _____
   Sam: Oh really? I've seen that, it's great. Who are you going with?
   Yoko: _____
   Sam: (disappointed) Oh.
   Yoko: _____
   Sam: (brightly) Oh, that's all right then.

2. Tell students to keep their textbooks shut. Ask students to read the cloze dialogue and then try to fill in the blanks.
3. Play the dialogue to the students as they check what they have written with what they actually hear.
4. Ask students to check their answers against the dialogue in the textbook.

Caveats and Options

1. Omit several lines from both interlocutors rather than just one.
2. Ask students to read their dialogues to each other after they have finished the above.

Contributor

Dino Mahoney has lived and taught in Europe, the Middle East, and the Far East. He was Director of Studies for the British Council in Dubai and Hong Kong.

Riddle Listening

Levels
Advanced

Aims
Listen for key words
and phrases
Develop inferences on
the basis of these
Listen to and
understand poetry

Class Time
15 minutes

Preparation Time
Varies

Resources
Copy of a 20th century
poem

In this activity students listen to a poem and try to guess its title. The activity motivates the listener to listen to poetry attentively and to use key words and phrases to activate a schema revealing the subject or title of the poem. It presents poetry as a riddle to be solved. In this case, solving the riddle involves constructing a schema from key words and phrases in the poem, which allows for topic recognition.

Poems that can be used for this activity include "The Jaguar," by Ted Hughes; "The Forge," by Seamus Heaney; "The Archaeologist," by Peter Redgrove; "Empires," by Douglas Dunn, and "The Abortion," by Anne Sexton.

Procedure

1. Read the students the first verse or first few verses of a poem. Ask them to listen to the poem and try to identify the subject of the poem, which may also be its title. For example,

   I am silver and exact. I have no preconceptions.
   Whatever I see I swallow immediately
   Just as it is, unmisted by love or dislike.
   I am not cruel, only truthful—
   The eye of a little god, four cornered.
   Most of the time I meditate on the opposite wall.
   It is pink, with speckles. I have looked at it so long
   I think it is a part of my heart. But it flickers.
   Faces and darkness separate us over and over.
   (Sylvia Plath, "Mirror," Verse 1)

2. Ask students to share their ideas of the title/topic of the poem in pairs. Ask them to try to give reasons for their ideas.

3. Read the second or subsequent verses and ask the students to listen and try to confirm their hypotheses.

4. Ask students to confer once more in pairs about the title, and then hand out copies of the poem with the title on it.

Caveats and Options

1. Record the poem and play it in short chunks. At each pause ask students, in pairs, to speculate what the title/subject is. Once you have finished, play the poem in its entirety for students to confirm their hypotheses.

2. Use poems that mention their topic/title only once and, when reading the poem leave a silence where the word should be. For example, in Walter De La Mare's poem, "Snow," the word *snow* is only mentioned once, so it is easy to omit without disrupting the reading.

3. If one is available use a recording of the actual poet reading the poem.

Contributor

Dino Mahoney has lived and taught in Europe, the Middle East, and the Far East. He was Director of Studies for the British Council in Dubai and Hong Kong.

Headlines

Levels
High
beginning–intermediate

Aims
Develop extensive and
intensive listening skills

Class Time
25 minutes

Preparation Time
10–15 minutes

Resources
Short, recently recorded
news program from the
radio or TV

This activity helps students develop the ability to use existing knowledge to help them understand the unknown.

Procedure

1. Elicit information about what has been in the news recently.
2. Elicit what the students expect to be the main headlines and write their suggestions on the board. You may want to use this stage to preteach any difficult vocabulary, for example,

   Students: What do you call it when the earth moves?
   Teacher: *Earthquake*

3. Play the first part of the taped news when the headlines are given. Ask students to listen to the tape and see if their suggestions were correct. Have the students discuss in pairs any differences between their suggestions and those they heard on the tape. Check the headlines with, the class.
4. Play the whole news program and ask the students to listen and make short notes for each news item, for example,

   Earthquake—Japan—no one killed—lots of damage—6.5.

(With lower-level students you may need to pause the tape after each news item or play the tape more than once so that they can take notes.)

5. Ask students to retell the news stories to each other, using their notes.

Contributors

Jackie Wheeler is a Lecturer at Sir Robert Black College of Education, Hong Kong. Austin Conway is Language Instructor at the Hong Kong University of Science and Technology.

Here's Half the News

Levels
Intermediate +

Aims
Practice listening for
specific information
Predict what is going to
be said

Class Time
20 minutes

Preparation Time
10–15 minutes

Resources
Audiotaped news
bulletin from radio in
two versions: one
complete and another
with only the beginning
of the report but not the
end

People often listen to the news on the radio while doing other things: driving a car, eating breakfast, talking to a friend. This activity helps students fill in the missing parts of a news report by guessing what was said.

Procedure

1. Have a general chat about the current news with the students as a warm-up exercise.
2. Divide the class into groups and give each group a name or number (see Miller, 1994). Tell the students that you are going to play a game and that they can score points for their group according to how well they play the game.
3. To familiarize the students with the game have a trial run. Play one half of a news report, for example, "From Ethiopia reports are coming in a severe draught which is affecting most of the country. Our reporter has said that more than half the . . . ." Ask the class what kind of information might be in the other half of the sentence and how the report might continue. Write up the suggestions on the board. Play the report again and, when it stops, give the class an example of how to continue, using ideas from the board. For example,

   From Ethiopia reports are coming in of a severe drought which is affecting most of the country. Our reporter has said that more than half the population is suffering because of the draught and that there is a shortage of most food-stuff. The country's president has appealed for aid.

4. Play the next report and, when it stops, ask someone from one of the groups to continue the report. If the student nominated responds quickly and with relevant information to complete the report, give

85

the student five points. If there is hesitation, irrelevant information, or not enough information, prompting from the student group, give the student fewer points (allocating the points should be done in a lighthearted way). Do not tell the students in advance who you are going to ask to complete the report so that they all listen to each section.

5. Once you have played the game and tallied up the points, play the complete version of the news report. Play the items one at a time and ask the students in their groups to discuss what was similar to the student version and what was different.

Caveats and Options

1. Have the students predict all the headlines first, then listen to see which group got the most.
2. Elicit vocabulary for each type of news item and write them on the board. Students have to use at least five of the words on the board in their report.

Reference and Further Reading

Miller, L. (1994). Arranging students into groups using vocabulary. In P. Nation (Ed.), *New Ways in teaching vocabulary* (pp. 8–10). Alexandria, VA: TESOL.

Contributor

Julie Wilkinson is a teacher at the British Council, Bangkok, and has several years' experience teaching in England, France, and Greece.

Part II: Developing Listening With Other Skills

♦ Listening and Speaking
Folk and Fairy Tales: Find the Changes

Levels
High beginning +

Aims
Identify mistakes in a
known text

Class Time
25–45 minutes

Preparation Time
5 minutes

Resources
Folk or fairy tale known
to the learners

The content of folk and fairy tales can motivate students. When learners are dealing with a story they already know, understanding the English becomes easier. However, just telling them the story provides no real task. In this activity, identifying changes in the content becomes the goal. The activity leads into a speaking/listening activity in which the learners come up with their own variations of known stories, practice them, then tell—and listen to—their partner's stories.

Procedure

1. Choose a short folk or fairy tale that all the students know. Decide on several changes you could make in the story. For example, if you were to tell the Little Red Riding Hood story, you could change the color of her clothes, have books rather than food in the basket, have the villain be a bear instead of a wolf, and so on.
2. In class, tell the story. Learners listen to the story and write down all your "mistakes" (changes).
3. After they've finished with your story, have the class brainstorm a list of well-known folk or fairy tales. Write the list on the board.
4. Show the learners how to make a story skeleton. This is similar to an outline of the story but doesn't follow a precise outlining format. Instead, it is a list of short items indicating the main events in the story. The items should usually not be complete sentences. A skeleton for Little Red Riding Hood might begin like this:

   little girl—red cape—went to Grandma's house—basket of goodies— forest—met wolf . . . .

5. Have learners in pairs choose a story from the brainstormed list and write a skeleton for it.
6. Have the students decide on three or more changes they could make to their story and practice telling the story, including the changes.
7. Recombine the learners so everyone has a new partner. In turns, have them tell their version of the story as partners listen and try to identify the changes.

Caveats and Options

1. The story skeleton technique is from Morgan and Rinvolucri (1983). Making story skeletons is useful as, even with well-known stories, the students may not have thought about the stories for many years (much less tell them in a foreign language). Even in the native culture, it is easy to forget parts of the stories. Many native English speakers, for example, if asked to retell *Romeo and Juliet,* would come up with something like this: "Their families are feuding. There's a big part. Romeo and Juliet fall in love. Then, uh, uh, some stuff happens and they kill themselves." Preparing the skeleton allows learners to remember the story and supports them because they can use it for reference when they tell the story.
2. In ESOL situations, the learners will most likely all know some of the same stories from their own culture. In mixed-culture ESOL classes, start with a story known nearly everywhere or with a text the students have previously heard or read. If there are not enough known stories to do the second part of the activity as "find the changes," skip Step 3. Have learners do a skeleton of any story they know from their own culture. Without changing it. At Step 8, partners simply listen and write at least three things about the story.

References and Further Reading

Morgan, J., & Rinvolucri, M. (1983). *Once upon a time.* Cambridge: Cambridge University Press.

Contributors

Steven Brown is Curriculum Coordinator at the University of Pittsburgh English Language Institute in the United States. Marc Helgesen is Associate Professor at Miyagi Gakuin Women's College, Sendai, Japan. They are coauthors of Active Listening *series (Cambridge University Press) and the* New English Firsthand *series (Longman/Lingual House).*

Pair Story

Levels
High beginners +

Aims
Develop skills in
reproducing received
speech
Encourage interactive
learning

Class Time
30–40 minutes

Preparation Time
20 minutes

Resources
Short, lively stories

Students can benefit from interactive activities designed to improve listening and speaking skills.

Procedure

1. Copy stories appropriate for the proficiency level, a different story for each pair of students.
2. Place students in pairs and give a story to one partner in each pair, who serves as the "teacher." The other student is the "student."
3. Tell the teacher not to show the story to the student. The teacher must read the story and *tell* it (no oral reading) to the student. The student is free to ask for clarification and as many repetitions of the story as he/she needs.
4. The student practices telling the story, with the teacher coaching and correcting, including help with pronunciation and expressiveness.
5. When the teacher is satisfied that the student is ready, the student tells the story to the class.
6. If you give grades, consider expressiveness, sequence, accuracy of content, and completeness. The teacher and the student receive the same grade.

Caveats and Options

1. Use short, factual articles. Newspapers are good sources.
2. Ask students to tell folk stories from their native countries.

References and Further Reading

Hill, L. A. (1965) *Elementary stories for reproduction*. Oxford: Oxford University Press.

Hill, L. A. (1980) *Intermediate anecdotes in American English*. New York: Oxford University Press.

Hill, L. A. (1981) *Advanced anecdotes in American English*. New York: Oxford University Press.

Contributor

Gaye Childress is Curriculum Coordinator and Teacher Trainer for instruction in reading, listening, and speaking at the Intensive English Language Institute at the University of North Texas, Denton, in the United States.

While You Were Out . . .

Levels
Any

Aims
Practice giving and taking down phone messages
Practice the language of asking for repetition and clarification as well as reported speech

Class Time
30 minutes

Preparation Time
None

Resources
Dummy phones (either old, broken ones or training phones used by some businesses, phone companies)

Procedure

1. Get a pad of telephone message slips that can be ripped off and given to individual students.
2. You may want to tell the students one class in advance to think of several messages they could give to someone over the phone in order to save time on the day of the actual activity.
3. Hand out the telephone message slips and clarify that the students understand how to use them, including any relevant vocabulary (e.g., *urgent*).
4. If the students have not already done so for homework, have them note down the messages that they are going to give to someone else (including the name, either a student in the class or a fictitious individual).
5. Go over the conventions of answering a phone and taking a message, for both a residence and a business.
6. Divide the class into pairs. Depending on how many messages each student is going to give, either have students work in the same pairs for the activity or switch pairs part way through.
7. In pairs, have the students take turns "calling" each other and leaving a message for someone else.
8. After the message has been taken down, the two students compare the message to the original to make sure it was relayed correctly.

Caveats and Options

1. If you want to practice reported speech, the student who took down the message can tell it to another student (especially if it is the person that the message was addressed to).

2. You could also do the party game version of this, where the message is passed down a line of people, without writing it down, and then the final version of the message is compared with the original.

Contributor

Mark Dickens teaches at Fields College International, Victoria, Canada.

The Joe Show

Levels
Low intermediate +

Aims
Practice speaking,
listening, and note-
taking skills while
students learn about
one another

Class Time
10–15 minutes to gather
information
Two 50-minute class
periods for the show

Preparation Time
1 hour

Resources
Prepared interview
questions for each
student
Spotlight
Cassette player
Cassette of upbeat TV
music
A few jokes
Talk-show host/hostess-
style clothing
A room that can be
slightly darkened

In this activity students are guests on a TV talk show. A talk show is an excellent way to learn about a person, and the students will be able to learn a lot about their fellow classmates from this activity. They will practice speaking skills when it is their turn to be interviewed. They will practice listening skills while being attentive members of the "studio audience." They will practice note-taking skills as they take notes on each guest for a subsequent "Joe Show Quiz," featuring the exciting stories of the many fabulous guest stars who have appeared on "The Joe Show."

Procedure

1. Spend 10–15 minutes at the end of a class gathering information about your students. In addition to getting their names, birthdays, nationalities, occupations, hobbies, and family information, ask them about things that might elicit interesting anecdotes: What is the funniest, strangest, most dangerous, or most embarrassing thing that has ever happened to you, or that has happened since arriving in this country? Is someone in your family or someone you know famous or eccentric? What do you hope to do in your future? Use this information to design questions for interviews. Also, prepare one or two jokes to use in your "opening monologue" routine.
2. Calm any fears by assuring students that they will be asked questions only about what they have written about themselves. Clearly convince the students of the reasons for doing this activity and they will then allow themselves to be caught up in the tongue-in-cheek spirit of it.
3. Before the next class starts, dress up in your finest talk-show garb and set up the classroom so that it resembles a television talk show studio. Hire one student to be your sound engineer and another to be your lighting technician.

4. Remind students of the reasons for the exercise and tell them to be ready with pencil and paper to take notes.

5. Darken the room and stand in the doorway. The sound engineer starts the tape. When the music begins, the lighting technician flashes the "spotlight" on and off as you flash the overhead lights on and off. Announce in your best TV announcer's voice:

Ladies and gentlemen, it is time once again for another exciting hour of 'The Joe ___ Show' featuring exciting guests from around the world. (Applause) And now, a ___ warm welcome for the star of our show . . . . Ladies and gentlemen, here's Joe. (Much applause)

Come running and waving on to the "stage." Shake hands with a few people. Point at someone and smile in delightful recognition as if spotting an old friend you haven't seen in a while. Laugh to yourself. Bow. When the music ends, be sure the tape is turned off and the spot light is turned on.

6. Thank and welcome the audience to the show. Tell a joke or two. Then introduce the first guest—pick the most outgoing member of the class for this hot spot. Ensure she receives applause. Have the student sign her name on "The Celebrity Sign-In" on the chalkboard. Interview the guest. While doing so, maintain the facade of television by saying things like: "Do you watch 'The Joe Show' every week in Italy (or wherever)? It's nice to have you on the show. I know you've got a busy schedule, so it was so kind of you to drop by and spend some time with us today." Repeat with another guest.

7. After the second interview, take a "commercial break" so you can check on students' notes. A few might have completely forgotten to take notes. Others' notes may be too meager or in complete sentence form. Advise them accordingly. When you go to and come back from a commercial, be sure to use your theme music. Also do so at the end of each show. (Should you finish early, have the students compare notes and clarify any confusion with the "guest stars" directly.)

8. In the next class, give "The Joe Show Quiz" using information about the students from their interviews. It is far easier to devise questions after each class for those students just interviewed than it is to wait

until the end of the 2-day activity, when things discussed earlier are no longer so fresh in one's memory. Carry over the show biz atmosphere into the quiz by beginning with your theme music and writing and reading the instructions in a television announcer voice. Collect, correct, record, and return the quiz. Go over the answers by calling the number of a question and having that student read the answer about herself.

Contributor

Joseph R. Fraher has an MA in TEF/SL from San Francisco State University in the United States. He has performed "The Joe Show" for the past 8 years. He currently teaches in Japan.

Quietball

Levels
Beginning +; children

Aims
Develop listening and
speaking skills within
student-student
interaction

Class Time
7–10 minutes

Preparation Time
Minimal

Resources
Soft ball
Picture cards for
beginning students

This activity helps to increase students' independence and sense of achievement by encouraging them to communicate with one another in the target language.

Procedure

1. Remind students that only the person holding the ball is allowed to talk.
2. Hold the ball, ask a question, call a student's name, and throw the ball to the student.
3. The student catches the ball, answers the question, "I don't know," and asks another student the question ("I don't know, Kenji, what is the capital of North Dakota?" is an acceptable answer.)
4. After answering the question, the second student repeats the process.

Caveats and Options

Use specific topics (provided by picture cards), or, for more advanced students, leave the topics unspecified.

Contributor

Jennifer Hermes is a student in the MEd program at Temple University, Japan.

An Easy Introduction

Levels
False beginning

Aims
Relax while gaining confidence in listening comprehension ability
Greet instructor interactively

Class Time
15 minutes

Preparation Time
5 minutes

Resources
List of several questions often used at first meetings and their answers

The first time back in language class can be a terrifying time for students and an uncertain time for teachers trying to gauge their group's level. This idea uses the teacher's self-introduction as a way to relax students while letting teachers get a general grasp of the class's mood and skills.

Procedure

1. To get the adrenalin flowing, tell the class that you are going to give them a listening test of five questions with the answers in multiple choice. Give an example of the format with your name if necessary.

   What's my last name?   (a) Le   (b) Van   (c) Inoue

2. Ask the questions, giving hints so that students can answer even arcane personal questions. Students can answer any way you like: verbally, or in writing full sentences, in by letter or by a show of hands, and so forth.

   What does my sister do in her spare time?
   (a) plays tennis   (b) reads books   (c) watches TV   (d) play football

   (Hints: We don't have a TV. We live near a tennis court.)

Caveats and Options

1. Expand into a lesson about self-introductions by letting students write questions and answers about themselves and try them out on the class.
2. An adult class will enjoy questions that stump them or force them to answer by inference and make use of their world knowledge. For example, as I look Oriental and have Canadian nationality, I often ask students where was I born and give them choices ranging from Nepal to England.

3. This idea is an aural use of the standard multiple-choice format. You can easily use it as an icebreaker or an enjoyable check for more difficult materials.

Contributor

Van Le is Instructor at the Japan Intercultural Academy of Municipalities. She has edited Hands on Team Teaching (Hokkaido AJET), *a collection of teaching ideas for language teaching ideas in Japanese. Her interests include English as an international language, computer-assisted instruction, and intercultural education.*

Multilevel Interaction

Levels
Any

Aims
Interact with one
another
Improve spoken
language skills

Class Time
10–20 minutes

Preparation Time
5 minutes

Resources
An advertisement that
includes people as well
as the product being
sold (e.g., a car)

Students learn at different rates and employ various strategies; they may also acquire different skills, resulting in a group with some members who are very proficient in reading, and others who read poorly but speak quite well.

In these exercises, the focus is on the message rather than on a specific set of grammar points. The students at various levels can understand the material in different ways ranging from what sort of material it is (lower levels) to what specific details it contains (middle to higher levels).

Procedure

1. Reproduce the advertisement or allow the whole class to see it as a poster.
2. Lower levels give a basic description of the product—size,color, and number of people in the advertisement. If the target structure is *be* and the advertisement is for a car, ask questions about the people in the advertisement and about the shape, color, model, and age of the car. Ask whether it is a truck or car and whether it is expensive.
3. Have middle levels do Step 2, then add verbs to describe what the people are doing (or will do or have done). Ask "Will you buy the product? How much will you pay? Do you like it?"
4. Have higher levels do Step 3, then discuss the roles the product plays in the United States or in the home culture. After the oral work students can write their own impressions or read an article related to the product. For example, they may find something about cars and transportation, home electronics, or computers.

Caveats and Options

Using newspapers of magazines, have the class choose news items, form small groups, decide on an item, and make a short presentation to the class. Guidelines for the presentation follow.

1. Low levels: Look at the headline. Who is Mr._____? (e.g., President. Prime Minister, Banker)
2. Middle levels: Read the article. Who is Mr. X? What did he do? Where? When? Where? Why? Change the paragraph to the present as if you are observing the event now.
3. Higher levels: Summarize the news article in your own words. Describe a similar event in your own experience. Write a letter to the editor in response to the article.

References and Further Reading

A thematic approach using real target culture materials is shown in Bragger and Rice (1984) (French example). Other discussions can be found in Krashen (1983) and Dunkel (1986).

Bragger, J. D., & Rice, D. B. (1984) *Allons-y! Le français par etapes.* Boston: Heinle & Heinle.

Dunkel, C. (1986) Developing listening fluency in L2: Theoretical principles and pedagogical considerations. *Modern Language Journal*, *70*, 99-106.

Krashen, S. D., & Terrell, T. D. (1983). *The natural approach.* Oxford: Pergamon.

Contributor

Douglas R. Magrath teaches ESOL at Seminole Community College, in Florida, in the United States. He has also conducted ESOL workshops for Volusia County, Florida. He has published in Foreign Language Annals, Selected Articles From the TESOL Newsletter, *and* Teaching English to Deaf and Second Language Students.

Chain Story

Levels
High beginning +

Aims
Listen for logical
connectors in a story
Order information

Class Time
10 minutes

Preparation Time
30 minutes

Resources
One paragraph cut up
into sentences

This activity shows students how information is ordered and how connectors are often used in this process.

Procedure

1. Find, or write, a suitable paragraph for the level of your students that has information in order. The following is an example for a beginning class:

   Bob gets up a 7 o'clock every morning. First, he washes his face. Then he eats breakfast. After breakfast, Bob gets dressed. He leaves his house at 8 a.m. Bob walks to the bus stop. He takes the number 72 bus to the train station. Then he catches a train to the city. Bob starts work at 9 o'clock.

2. Cut up the paragraph into sentences.
3. Give a sentence to each member of a group, or the class. Tell the students to memorize the sentence. Take the sentences from the students.
4. Ask the students to form a circle. Have each student say the sentence out loud. By listening to each others' sentences the students should order themselves into the story.
5. Get the students to say the story out loud in the order it was written.

Caveats and Options

With advanced students, use a story that is quite complex, perhaps with different orders possible. Have the students reorder themselves as many times as possible, each time listening to the complete story to see if it makes sense.

Contributor

Lindsay Miller is a Lecturer in the English Department of City University of Hong Kong. He has taught EFL in Europe, the Middle East, and Southeast Asia.

The Radio English Show

Levels
Any

Aims
Encourage students to
listen to English outside
of class and make their
own cassettes.
Reinforce collaborative
learning

Class Time
10 minutes

Preparation Time
None

Resources
Audiotape recorder

Students frequently do not have sufficient opportunity to practice their listening skills outside of the class, especially at lower levels. The activity described here focuses their attention on a homework task that tries to overcome this problem while enlarging their vocabulary and entertaining them.

Procedure

1. Demonstrate the process of making a cassette interactively by taking a tape player into class and interviewing some of the students: "This is Radio English and today we are going to interview people about smoking cigarettes. What do you think about smoking?" (or some other topic you think the class will be interested in). After the first person answers, hit the pause button and ask the next person. When they start to answer, release the pause, and hit it again when they finish. Then continue asking students until you have enough answers to make about 5 minutes of recording time.
2. Immediately play the tape for the students to listen to. Apart from letting the students listen to their classmates' voices on tape (which they love), ask the class to listen for any unfamiliar words or expressions. When there is an unknown word or expression, ask the students to find out from each other, or from the person who used the expression, what it means.
3. Tell the class that you have just made an English Radio Show cassette in only 10 minutes. Explain to the class that for homework you want each member of the class to make an English Radio Show cassette and bring it to the next class. Tell them to ask any question they want, to interview several people in English, and to make a tape of about

5 minutes (the students usually choose to interview each other, which makes listening to the tape afterwards more enjoyable for them).

4. At the next lesson ask the students to write their name on the cassette they have brought. Then have the students exchange tapes so that everyone has a different cassette tape. The next homework task is to listen to the new tape. If there are any new words or expressions, the students should make an attempt to find out what it means. At the next lesson they can check some of the new words or expressions with the owner of the tape.

5. Repeat the procedure as many times as you want.

Contributor

Tim Murphey teaches at Nanzan University in Nagoya, Japan.

Directed Listening-Thinking Activity

Levels
Intermediate +

Aims
Be introduced to the
use of listening
strategies
Listen interactively

Class Time
30–45 minutes

Preparation Time
20 minutes

Resources
An appropriate audio
recording (e.g., see
References and Further
Reading)
A portable cassette
player equipped with a
pause button

This activity builds upon a widely implemented L2 reading procedure known as *the directed reading-thinking activity* (DRTA) (see Gunderson, 1991). ESOL learners who receive instruction in DRTA procedures have opportunities to practice interacting with textual material via prediction, sampling, and confirmation strategies. Three questions that L2 teachers ask to facilitate students' engagements with DRTA procedures are the following: (a) What do you think this selection is about? (b) What information or ideas do you think will be coming next? and (c) What makes you think so? This activity illustrates one way of introducing students to a similar procedure while focusing upon the L2 listening, rather than the L2 reading, process (see Lebauer, 1984; Murphy, 1991).

Procedure

1. Select a commercially available audio recording that seems appropriate for the proficiency levels and interests of the targeted group of ESOL learners, preferably one that is a monologue, a semistructured interview, or a minilecture. Examples are Dunkel and Pialorsi (1982), James (1992), Lebauer (1988), Lim and Smalzer (1989), Mason (1983), Roguski and Palmberg (1990), and Ruetten (1986). Preview it enough times to become generally aware of its content while avoiding overfamiliarity. Knowing the selection too well might stifle your spontaneous responses inside the classroom.
2. Begin to play the recording on the cassette player at the front of the room. As soon as the recording has begun to play, place a finger on the machine's pause button and prepare to press it down.
3. Following just a brief section of the initial portion of the passage (e.g., at the end of the speaker's first sentence), press the pause button.

4. Respond aloud to the initial section of the recording just been presented to the class, while illustrating DRTA type strategies for interacting with textual material. Some options are explaining to the class (a) what you think the listening selection is about (inferencing), (b) what ideas or information might be coming next (predicting), and (c) reasons for coming to these tentative impressions (sampling textual clues).

5. Release the pause button and play another brief section of the recording.

6. Repeat Steps 2–5 until the class has heard all of the listening selection. A 3-minute recording might be interrupted as many as a dozen different times. Interrupt the recording frequently but at natural breaks in the recorded speaker's delivery (e.g., immediately following a pause or hesitation, following an intonation shift that signals the completion of an idea, or prior to a change in topic development).

7. Have the students in the class discuss in small groups the content of the listening selection and your responses to it. Also in small groups, students can try recounting the topic's development while referring to their own written notes.

Caveats and Options

1. Have students recount the topic based upon a partial outline and/or participate in whole-class discussions about the topic. You can also encourage them to seek additional information about the topic outside of class.

2. Have the whole class complete a multiple-choice, short-answer, cloze, or brief essay assessment of their comprehension of the presentation.

3. In addition to the DLTA-type responses described above, you might also do one or more of the following while interacting with the listening selection:

   - summarize or paraphrase what everyone has just heard
   - expand upon an idea or piece of information presented in the recording
   - briefly define an unfamiliar word or phrase by discussing how it fits into the context of the topic being developed

- ask and try to answer a question that is suggested by information presented in the recording; offer a point of view in contrast to the recorded speaker's
- point out a sampled piece of information from the passage that either confirms or contradicts some earlier prediction of topic development
- briefly draw a connection between the content of the listening passage and your background knowledge

4. Once students are familiar with the procedure, have the members of the class do any, or all, of the above.
5. Reverse the focus of the entire procedure by soliciting interactive responses from students from the very beginning of the lesson while acting primarily as a facilitator.
6. During the interactive listening segment of the class, keep your responses to the selection as succinct as possible. The goal is to model the kinds of intrapersonal responses to listening materials that normally occur beneath the level of observable behavior but to do so for the whole class to hear. If you have too much to say it may distract students from their own developing interpretations and they may end up tuning out the recording completely and listening only to what you have to say. You might test out the procedure while interacting with a small group of friends, peer teachers, or other interested speakers of English.
7. Students can explore these or similar procedures for interactive listening on their own, in small groups, or with the whole class. Access to a number of different portable cassette players permits small groups of students to interact with listening selections as described above. Some modern language laboratory facilities may also be suitable for these purposes (see Murphy, 1992, 1993).
8. Some students might be interested in generating their own recordings by taping brief segments of audio material from commercial radio, short-wave, or television broadcasts. When working with such self-selected materials, individual students could plan to present a segment of their own recording in a small group (or to the whole class) while following an interactive listening procedure. There are restrictions

upon the legitimate use of "off-air" broadcasts of these kinds, even when used for instructional purposes (see Otto, 1989; Reed & Stanek, 1986, or *The Official Fair-Use Guidelines,* 1985, for guidelines on the use of such materials in classroom settings and related copyright considerations).

References and Further Reading

Dunkel, P., & Pialorsi, F. (1982). *Advanced listening comprehension: Developing aural and note-taking skills*. New York: Newbury House.

Gunderson, L. (1991). *ESL literacy instruction: A guidebook to theory and practice*. Englewood Cliffs, NJ: Prentice Hall.

James, G. (1992). *Interactive listening on campus*. Boston, MA: Heinle & Heinle.

Lebauer, R. S. (1984). Using lecture transcripts in EAP lecture comprehension courses. *TESOL Quarterly, 18*, 41–54.

Lebauer, R. S. (1988). *Learn to listen; Listen to learn: An advanced ESOL lecture comprehension and note-taking textbook*. Englewood Cliffs, NJ: Prentice Hall.

Lim, P., & Smalzer, W. (1989). *Noteworthy: Listening and note taking skills*. New York: Newbury House.

Mason, A. (1983). *Understanding academic lectures*. Englewood Cliffs, NJ: Prentice Hall.

Murphy, J. M. (1991). Oral communication in TESOL: Integrating speaking, listening and pronunciation. *TESOL Quarterly, 25*, 51–71.

Murphy, J. M. (1992). From caterpillar to butterfly: Using modern technology within the current paradigm of ESOL instruction. *TESL Canada Journal, 9*, 80–98.

Murphy, J. M. (1993). Using modern technological resources for communicative purposes. *TESOL Journal, 2*, 11–14.

The official fair-use guidelines. (1985). Friday Harbor, WA: Copyright Information Services.

Otto, S. (1989). The language laboratory in the computer age. In W. Flint Smith (Ed.), *Modern technology in foreign language education: applications and projects* (pp. 12–41). Lincolnwood, IL: National Textbook Co.

Reed, M. H., & Stanek, D. (1986). Library and classroom use of copyrighted videotapes and computer software. *American Libraries, 17*, A–D.

Roguski, C., & Palmberg, E. (1990). *Academic mini-lectures: A text for listening and note-taking practice*. New York: Maxwell Macmillan.

Ruetten, M. (1986). *Comprehending academic lectures*. New York: Macmillan.

Contributor

John M. Murphy is Assistant Professor of Applied Linguistics and ESOL at George State University in the United States where he prepares ESOL teachers. His publications have appeared in the TESOL Quarterly, English for Specific Purposes, TESL Canada Journal, Foreign Language Annals, Journal of Second Language Writing, *and* TESOL Journal.

Interrupted Story

Levels
Beginning +

Aims
Listen for cues and
descriptions

Class Time
30 minutes

Preparation Time
20 minutes

Resources
Short story that has
various nouns (more
than one story may be
used for different
groups)

In this activity students have to practice cueing into specific information and selecting what is important in a description.

Procedure

1. Divide the class into groups of six or eight.
2. Give one student in each group a story to read. Give each of the other members of the group a picture of something mentioned in the story (e.g., a room, a car, a person, a building).
3. Give the students some time to think about how they are going to describe the picture.
4. Tell the students with the story to begin reading and to continue reading until interrupted by one of the members of the group. The group listens to the story. When they hear a reference to the picture they have, they interrupt the speaker and describe the picture (only the student describing the picture should be able to see it). This description can be given more than once, depending on how often a reference is made to in the story. For example, the story line might be something like:

Mr. Smith (interruption—description of Mr. Smith) lives in a house (interruption—description of house) with his wife (interruption—description of wife) and a dog (interruption—description of dog). Everyday he takes his dog (interruption . . .) for a walk in the park near his home. On his way to the park he passes a very unusual building (interruption . . .) . . . and so on.

5. After the story has been completed, ask one member of the group to retell the story, adding some descriptions where necessary, to the rest of the class. Have the class listen and correct the storyteller if necessary.

Contributor

Elizabeth A. Price is a freelance ESOL teacher. She lives in Edinburgh, Scotland.

Memory Dictation

Levels
Low intermediate +

Aims
Listen for information
and ordering of events

Class Time
30 minutes

Preparation Time
20 minutes

Resources
Copy of three different
texts (short stories)

This activity challenges students so that they have to use different learning strategies.

Procedure

1. Affix to the board three different stories. The length and complexity of the text will depend on the level of your students and/or what you want the students to focus on.
2. Pair the students up. One is A, the other is B.
3. Tell the As to sit away from the board and have a sheet of paper and pencil ready.
4. Tell the Bs to go to the board and begin reading the stories. Tell the Bs to select the story they like most.
5. Have the Bs read parts of the story and commit them to memory before going to their partner and dictating the story to them. A listens and writes the story down. If A hears any inconsistencies in the story line or has difficulty understanding what B says, B returns to the board to check that part of the story again.
6. Once A has the complete story, A reads it to B, who listens and makes a final check from the board.
7. After all the pairs have finished their memory dictations read out the stories, or have them recorded on tape to play to the class, so that everyone can check their written version.

Caveats and Options

Cut up the texts and put the paragraphs put on the board so that the reader/speaker has to decide which paragraphs to memorize and dictate to A.

Contributor

Elizabeth A. Price is a freelance ESOL teacher. She lives in Edinburgh, Scotland.

Picture Storytelling

Levels
Any

Aims
Listening for pleasure

Class Time
Varies

Preparation Time
20 minutes

Resources
A selection of
photographs or pictures
balanced among
people, buildings,
animals, interesting
objects, weather

Storytelling is a part of everyday experience. This activity helps students practice telling a story.

Procedure

1. Affix the pictures or photographs to the board. Make sure that all the students can see what the pictures are about.
2. Elicit some relevant vocabulary about the pictures from the students. For people you must ask, "What does she look like?" "What kind of person is she?" " What's her job?" "What hobbies does she have?" For buildings you must ask, "What kind of building is this?" " Who works in it?" "How could you describe it?"
3. Form the students into groups of four or five. Have them create a story together using the pictures for ideas. They should not write anything down but create the story orally. Have the students practice telling the story to each other until they feel that they know it well.
4. Re-form the students into different groups so that one student from each of the old groups is in the new group. Inform the students that they have to retell their stories to each other.
5. Take a vote to find out which story the students liked the most and why.

Contributor

Elizabeth A. Price is a freelance ESOL teacher. She lives in Edinburgh, Scotland.

Group Dictation Race

Levels
Any

Aims
Encourage cooperation
Develop grammatical
accuracy in listening
comprehension and
transfer this to writing
skills
Review or introduce
vocabulary or reduced
forms

Class Time
25 minutes +

Preparation Time
Varies

Resources
Chalkboard and chalk
Paper and pencils
Several short dictation
passages

Many teachers find dictation useful for teaching and assessment purposes, but individual dictations are often tedious exercises. This activity, while maintaining the same teaching goals as traditional dictations, creates a livelier atmosphere by including group cooperation and intergroup competition in the task.

Procedure

1. Divide the class into small groups. Assign each group a section of the chalkboard. Give each group one, two, or three pieces of chalk.
2. Read a dictation (sentence or paragraph). Have students write what they hear on a piece of paper.
3. After one or two readings, instruct the students to compare the individual dictations with those of their group members.
4. Have each group come up with one single version.
5. Ask each group to send one "scribe" to the appropriate section of the chalkboard. That person then writes the one dictation the group has decided on.
6. As soon a group finishes writing on the board, make marks next to the lines with errors and allow time for the group to discuss what the errors might be before they correct them.
7. When a group's dictation is correct, direct the entire class's attention to it.
8. Read the correct version of the dictation, pointing to words or reduced forms as they are pronounced, if desired.
9. Award points to each group depending on the accuracy of their dictation then move on to another dictation.

Caveats and Options

To change the focus to punctuation, write or choose a dictation with easy words but complex sentences and ask the students to put in the punctuation themselves.

Contributor

Cindy Mckeag Tsukamoto is an Assistant Professor of English as a Second Language at Roosevelt University, Chicago in the United States. She is the coauthor, with Sally La Luzerne-Oi, Tell Me About It! *(Heinle & Heinle).*

Interrupt Me If I Am Wrong

Levels
Intermediate +

Aims
Practice interrupting
speakers when they are
wrong

Class Time
20–30 minutes

Preparation Time
20 minutes

Resources
Any picture that is clear
and simple enough to
be described

In this activity the teacher gives the students wrong information to see if they notice that it is wrong. The activity also provides practice in taking the initiative to interrupt, one of the most difficult actions for some students because of their cultural background.

Procedure

1. As a prelistening activity you may want to teach some phrases that students can use to interrupt, such as "Excuse me . . .," "Just a moment, please . . . ."
2. Find a simple and clear picture to describe.
3. Show the picture to the students.
4. Describe the picture correctly: There is a tree on the left side and three birds are flying over the tree. The sun is shining. One car is parking in the middle and two flowers are blooming on the right side.
5. Explain to the students that you will now describe the picture incorrectly.
6. Ask the students to interrupt you and provide the correct information: Teacher: "There is one tree on the right side . . . ." The student is expected to interrupt at this point, "Excuse me, there are two flowers on the right side."
7. Continue to describe the picture incorrectly until the students find all the incorrect information.

Caveats and Options

You can be do this activity in pairs or in small groups. To emphasize speaking skills, have the students themselves describe the picture incorrectly.

Contributor

Michiko Usui is a student in the MEd in TESOL program at Temple University, Japan.

Attending to Conversation

Levels
Intermediate +

Aims
Develop skills in
attending/listening
Develop skill in
summarizing orally what
the speaker has said

Class Time
40–50 minutes

Preparation Time
20 minutes

Resources
None

In this exercise, L2 learners participate in conversation actively as both speaker and listener. It contributes to improvement of the learner's fluency and confidence.

Procedure

1. Explain the objectives of this exercise (the students will be aware of the roles of speaker and listener, and they will try to become good listeners; the students, being good listeners, will summarize orally what the speaker has said).
2. Put students into a speaker-listener pairs, or groups of 3 or 4 if the class size is more than 12. In case of groups, assign students to be speaker(s) and listeners.
3. Explain to students that the listener should attend to the conversation as much as possible.
4. Explain the strategies for attending to a conversation, such as asking questions and/or using fillers.
5. List and let students practice the words and expressions that can be used to attend to conversations (e.g., *Uh uh, Is it? What do you mean by . . .*).
6. Give instructions before letting students start the conversation.

   The listener should control the topic, try to ask as many questions as possible of the speaker, and give as many fillers to the speaker. The speaker should speak or answer the questions but not ask questions of the listener (i.e., there is no turn taking in this exercise).

7. Let the conversation begin. The listener selects a topic and initiates the conversation.

8. After letting the students have the conversation for 10 minutes, stop the activity.
9. Ask the listener of each pair or group to summarize what the speaker has said.
10. Discuss *attending* and compare it with the real-life situations.

Caveats and Options

Audiotape the conversation and let the students analyze it (see also Curran, 1983).

References and Further Reading

Acton, W. (1984). Attending skills for ESOL students. *American Language Journal, 2,* 17–37.

Goffman, E. (1976). Replies and responses. *Language in Society, 5,* 257–313.

Curran, C. (1983). Counseling-learning. In J. W. Oller, Jr., & P. A. Richard-Amato (Eds.), *Methods that work* (pp. 146–178). Rowley, MA: Newbury House.

Ivey, A. (1967). *Microcounseling*. New York: Applebaum.

Richard, J., & Schmidt, R. (1983). Conversational analysis. In J. Richards & R. Schmidt (Eds.), *Language and communication* (pp. 117–154). London: Longman.

Wardhaugh, R. (1985). *How conversation works*. Oxford: Basil Blackwell.

Contributor

Sayoko Okada Yamashita is Instructor of Japanese as an second language at International Christian University in Tokyo, Japan. She is the author of Textbook for JSL: Interview Projects for Intermediate to Advanced Japanese Learners, *(Kuroshio Publishers).*

◆ Listening and Pronunciation
Intonation Patterns in Questions

Levels
Intermediate–high
intermediate

Aims
Develop aural
discrimination skills in
recognizing rising and
falling intonation.
Encourage an
awareness in learners of
what such intonation
patterns signal to the
listener

Class Time
30 minutes

Preparation Time
30 minutes

Resources
Taped dialogue
prepared by the
instructor (or one from
a commercial tape, if
suitable)

In a taxonomy of listening skills compiled by Richards (1983), the "ability to recognize the functions of stress and intonation to signal the information structure of utterances" (p. 228) is listed as one of the microskills involved in conversational listening.

Procedure

1. Audiotape a dialogue (or select one available commercially) in which one speaker is asking questions and the other is providing short answers. A dialogue of a person making a report to a lost and found office would be particularly suitable (see Appendix); You can modify or change the topic of the conversation, however, at your discretion. Preparing various taped conversations will also enable you to use this activity more than once.
2. Prepare a line-by-line tapescript, leaving two or three spaces between lines so that students will have space to write.
3. Explain to the students that some forms of questions almost always have a falling intonation. Examples of such questions include

   - choice questions (*Should we go or should we wait here? Did he give it to you or did you buy it?*)
   - tag questions in which the speaker is actually seeking agreement (*It's hot today, isn't it? That was a good movie, wasn't it?*)
   - Wh-questions (*Where's the cat? Where can we catch the bus?*)

4. Explain that other types of questions almost always have a rising intonation. These include

   - yes/no questions (*Is she here yet? Did I get any mail?*)

- tag questions in which the speaker is seeking information (*You fed the dog, didn't you? Today is Friday, isn't it?*)
- confirmation questions (*Did you say 3:00? What did you say?*)

5. Play the tape for the students and tell them to draw arrows above the sentences (either up or down), depending on whether the sentence is spoken with a rising or falling intonation.
6. Play the tape again, pausing briefly after each line, to give the students a chance to make changes or corrections.
7. Ask the students to determine and write down which of the six question patterns (listed above) each of the questions belongs to.

Caveats and Options

1. You can modify this exercise for beginning-level students by focusing solely on the intonation patterns, and disregarding the meaning of the dialogue or the types of questions used.
2. A follow-up activity might involve having students work in pairs to produce their own dialogues and model them for the class. This would enable the students to practice articulation as well as aural discrimination.

References and Further Reading

Richards, J. C. (1983). Listening comprehension: Approach, design, procedure. *TESOL Quarterly, 17,* 219–240.

Appendix: A Sample Tapescript

Policeman: Can I help you, sir? (yes/no question)
Man: Yes, I've lost my wallet . . . . I'd like to make a report.

P: Your wallet? (Confirmation Question)
M: That's right . . . . I think I must have dropped it on the bus.

P: Which bus? (*wh*-question)
M: Excuse me? (confirmation question)

P: Which bus did you lose it on? (*wh*-question)

M: I'm not sure of the number. I think it was the 51. The 51 stops on Main Street, doesn't it? (tag question seeking information)

P: Yeah, that's the 51 all right . . . but did you get off near the library or the hospital? (choice question)
M: The hospital.

P: You were carrying some identification, weren't you? (tag question seeking agreement)
M: Yeah, I had my driver's license and a few credit cards.

P: How much money were you carrying? (*wh*-question)
M: Just about $10 fortunately . . . . I guess I should be glad that I wasn't carrying any more than that, shouldn't I? (tag questions seeking agreement)

P: Yeah, I'll say. Well, fill in this form and we'll call you if anyone turns it in.
M: Yeah, okay. Thanks a lot.

Contributor

Carol Biederstadt is an English instructor at Bunkyo Women's College in Tokyo, Japan.

Shadow Reading

Levels
Intermediate

Aims
Develop awareness of
English tone and
intonation patterns,
stress, and
pronunciation

Class Time
30–35 minutes

Preparation Time
30 minutes/conversation

Resources
Several taped
conversations from the
radio, preferably of
native speakers of
English

This activity requires students to listen to a taped conversation as they read aloud the transcript of the tape.

Procedure

1. Inform the students that this activity will enhance their ability to follow tone and intonation patterns, stress, and pronunciation in native English speech.
2. Briefly explain to the students what the tape is about.
3. Distribute the transcripts of the tape and ask the students to read over the transcripts. Clarify any problems of vocabulary.
4. Play the tape in sections; determine beforehand when to pause. Ask the students to follow the tape by reading the transcript aloud.
5. Pause the tape and let the students share their observations on the speech patterns they have just shadow-read. Repeat any section of special interest and ask the students to listen to the speaker.
6. After going through the tape section by section, rewind and ask the students to shadow-read the whole transcript along with the tape.

Caveats and Options

If this activity is done in a language laboratory, have the students record themselves reading the transcript onto a tape after completing the shadow-reading.

Contributor

Erlinda R. Boyle is Senior Instructor in the English Language Teaching Unit of the Chinese University of Hong Kong.

Comprehending Reduced Forms

Levels
Beginning +

Aims
Practice listening for the reduced forms produced by native speakers of American English

Class Time
Lessons: 5–10 minutes daily
Dictations: 15–20 minutes each

Preparation Time
Varies

Resources
Handout with reduced forms (see Appendix A)

We developed this idea while teaching for the UCLA/China Exchange Program at the Guangzhou English Language Center at Zhongshan University. As part of one course, we wanted to teach the students to understand the "real" language that they would encounter when they arrived in the United States. There was of course some difficulty in defining what we meant by *real*, but one theme that often recurred was that of connected speech, including contractions, elision, liaison, and reduction. We referred to these forms collectively as *reduced forms*.

Procedure

1. As part of each lesson, introduce some reduced forms. Write on the board the complete phrase. Then say the reduced form several times and write the reduced form next to the complete phrase. Once the students are used to listening to the reduced forms, say a new form and ask the students to try to write the correct form (this can be done by one student on the board or as a whole-class exercise).
2. At the end of each week, have a reduced-form dictation quiz. Tape several phrases in their reduced form and play the tape to the students. The students listen to the tape and try to write down the complete form of what is said (Appendix B). Scoring can be done only on the reduced forms (those underlined in Appendix B).

Caveats and Options

We created 10 such dictations to fit 10 groups of reduced forms that were taught during the 10 weeks of our curriculum. Both informally and formally (see Brown & Hilferty, 1986, 1987) we found that students' performances on the dictations were abysmal at the beginning of the course and considerably improved by the end of 10 weeks (e.g., on the order of 35% correct on average at the beginning and 61% by the end). We found these lessons both useful and popular among our students.

References and Further Reading

Brown, J. D., & Hilferty, A. (1986). Listening for reduced forms. *TESOL Quarterly, 20*, 759-763.

Brown, J. D., & Hilferty, A. (1987). The effectiveness of teaching reduced forms for listening comprehension. *RELC Journal, 17*, 59-70.

Brown, J. D., & Hilferty, A. (1989, January). Teaching reduced forms. *Modern English Teaching*, pp. 26-28.

Appendix A: Some American English Reduced Forms

Greetings
Howarya (How are you?)
   Howdy (How do you do?)
Farewells G'bye (Goodbye)
'bye (Goodbye)
Seeya (See you)
S'long (So long)
Modals + to
   goin'ta (going to)
   gonna (going to)
   gotta (got to)
   hafta (have to)
   otta (ought to)
   wanna (want to)
Modals + have
   coulda (could have)
   mighta (might have)
   shoulda (should have)
Negative Modals
   /wo/ [nasalized o] (won't)
   /do/ [nasalized o] (don't)
   duzn (doesn't)
   havn (haven't)

Other Combined Words
   c'mon (come on)
   g'won (go on)
   gedouda (get out of)
   wadda (what a)
Shortened Words
   'bout (about)
   'nother (another)
   'round (around)
   'cause (because)
   in' (-ing)
   jus' (just)
   ol' (old)
   yu (you)
   yer (your)
Words + Of
   kinda (kind of)
   sorta (sort of)
   type-a (type of)
   a lotta (a lot of)
   in fruna (in front of)
   ouda (out of)

Contractions

  N (or PN) + be (present)

  N (or PN) + be (future)

  N (or PN) + would

  N (or PN) + will

  N (or PN) + have (present)

  N (or PN) + have (past)

  Let + PN

  there + be

  there + have

  here + be

Question Forms

  Howza (How is the)

  How d'ya (How do you)

  How'd ja (How did you)

  How'ja (How would you)

Jawanna (Do you want to)

Yawanna (Do you want to)

Whaddya (What do you)

Whatduzzee (What does he)

Whaja (What did you)

Whaja (What would you)

Whad'll (What will)

Whatser (What is her)

Whatsiz (What is his)

Wheraya (Where are you)

When d'ya (When do you)

Where j'eat (Where did you eat?)

J'eat jet (Did you eat yet?)

J'ev (Did you have)

J'ever (Did you ever)

Wouldja (Would you)

Appendix B: A Sample Reduced-Forms Dictation

1. As it was read:

  Brian: Whenerya goin' ta Peking?

  Jim: I'm gonna go on Sunday.

  Brian: Boy! I wish I were gettin' ouda here fer awhile. Ya gotcher plane ticket?

  Jim: No. I've gotta gedit tomorrow.

  Brian: Whaddya hafta do in Peking?

  Jim: I've gotta giv'em some lectures. but I also wanna do some sightseeing.

  Brian: Where'll ya go?

  Jim: I wanna gedouda Peking 'n see the Great Wall.

  Brian: Okay. hav' a good time.

  Jim: Okay, g'bye.

2. As it was scored:

Brian: *When are you going to* Peking?
Jim: *I am going to* go on Sunday.

Brian: Boy! I wish I were *getting out of* here *for* awhile. *You got your* plane ticket?
Jim: No. I *have got to get it* tomorrow.

Brian: *What do you have to* do in Peking?
Jim: I *have got to give them* some lectures. but I also *want to* do some sightseeing.

Brian: *Where will you* go?
Jim: I *want to get out of* Peking *and* see the Great Wall.

Brian: Okay. *Have a* good time.
Jim: Okay, *goodbye*.

45 possible (counting italicized words only)

Contributors

James Dean Brown is on the graduate faculty of the Department of ESOL at the University of Hawaii at Manoa in the United States. He has published numerous journal articles as well as a book entitled Understanding Research in Second Language Learning *(Cambridge University Press). Ann G. Hilferty is currently doing doctoral work at Harvard University in the United States. Her publications include many journal articles and coauthorship of a book entitled* TESOL: Techniques and Procedures *(Newbury House).*

Teahouse Talk

Levels
Japanese high school students

Aims
Recognize auxiliary verb–pronoun reductions in common yes/no questions

Class Time
25–40 minutes

Preparation Time
30 minutes

Resources
List of auxiliary verb-pronoun combinations in both their written and reduced forms.
A list of 15–20 questions with the first two words missing.

Understanding indistinct word boundaries, reduced forms of words, and a variety of discoursal speeds are all microskills that Richards (1983) deems necessary for conversational listening. One of the most frequent types of rapid-speed reductions occurs when auxiliary verbs and pronouns are combined in yes/no questions.

Procedure

1. Distribute the sheet with the auxiliary verb-pronoun combinations and their reduced forms. Give the model pronunciation for each form and have students give a choral response. One possible way of representing these forms is listed below.

Can you	Kenya	Can't you	Can-cha
Did you	Did-ya	Didn't you	Din-cha
Will you	Will-ya	Won't you	Woon-cha
Do you	D'ya	Don't you	Doan-cha
Are you	Are-ya	Aren't you	Aren-cha
Were you	Were-ya	Weren't you	Weren-cha
Have you	Have-ya	Haven't you	Haven-cha
Can he	Kenny	Can't he	Can-nee
Did he	Diddee	Didn't he	Din-nee
Will he	Willie	Won't he	Woo-nee
Does he	Duzzy	Doesn't he	Duzzinee
Is he	Izzy	Isn't he	Izzinee
Was he	Wuzzy	Wasn't he	Wuzzinee
Has he	Hazzy	Hasn't he	Hazzinee
Can it	Kennit	Can't it	Can-nit
Did it	Diddit	Didn't it	Din-nit

Will it	Willit	Won't it	Woo-nit
Does it	Duzzit	Doesn't it	Duzzinit
Is it	Izzit	Isn't it	Izzinit
Was it	Wuzzit	Wasn't it	Wuzzinit
Has it	Hazzit	Hasn't it	Hazzinit

You can facilitate memorization of the most significantly reduced pronoun, *you*, by a simple mnemonic device. In negative questions *you* is generally reduced to *cha*, and in affirmative questions *you* usually becomes *ya*. *Cha* and *Ya* are Japanese readings of commonly used Chinese characters that can be combined to form the word *teahouse*.

2. Distribute the cloze exercise containing 15–20 questions with the first two words missing. Tell the students to put away their pronunciation sheets. Read each sentence several times with the teacher gradually slowing down but retaining the reduced forms as Ur (1987) recommends. Have students write the correct, unreduced forms in the blank spaces:

a. *Do you* speak Korean?
b. *Did you* come to school by train?
(Teacher's tapescript only)—How about your father?
c. *Does he* go to work by car?
d. *Can't he* play tennis?
e. *Will it* rain today?
f. *Weren't you* hungry this morning?

3. Have the students read the questions back to you in their reduced forms.
4. (Optional) Practice responding to these questions with a variety of answers. After giving examples, ask different groups to come up with two or three answers for each question. Then write a variety of appropriate responses on the chalkboard.

Caveats and Options

1. The focus of the combinations shouldn't exceed seven auxiliary verb forms and their variations (i.e., *did, can, will, do/does, have/has, were/was, and am/is/are*) nor seven pronouns (i.e., *I, you, he, she, it, we, and they*). Explicitly practicing the reduced forms of the pronouns *we, she, they,* and *I* will be unnecessary because it's generally not too difficult to recognize their reduced forms. Using a phonetic representation of the reduced forms rather than the phonetic alphabet will probably make it easier for the students to understand.

2. Confirm that students recognize that the questions "Can you swim?" and "Can't you swim?" require the same answer. In Japanese, these questions require different answers, and, in my experience, students frequently employ negative transfer when answering yes/no questions.

3. Auxiliary verb-pronoun reductions are also common in *wh*-questions. These questions are, of course, slightly longer and can be practiced once students have learned automatic processing of yes/no questions.

References and Further Reading

Richards, J. C. (1983). Listening comprehension: Approach, design, procedure. *TESOL Quarterly, 17,* 219–240.

Ur, P. (1987). *Teaching listening comprehension.* Cambridge: Cambridge University Press.

Contributor

Robert Cahill lives and works in Japan.

Angry, Sad, or Excited?

Levels
Beginning

Aims
Become aware of how
intonation contours and
stress patterns convey
meaning

Class Time
10 minutes

Preparation Time
5–10 minutes

Resources
Sample utterances (on
tape, if desired)

Students need to realize that pronunciation is not simply a matter of enunciating particular sounds correctly. Rhythm, stress, and intonation play a significant role in English in establishing the intended meaning.

Procedure

1. Write a list of adjectives such as the following on the board:

   happy angry sad excited sleepy
   bored frightened proud surprised questioning

2. Play the tape or read aloud the utterances. *What time is it? Where's my wallet? Please don't do that to me. I can't go to the party tonight. I didn't know it was so late.* If you read the utterances face the board so as not to give the students any paralinguistic clues.
3. Have the students write down the adjective that best characterize the emotional tone of each utterance.

Caveats and Options

1. Have students select short utterances from their textbook and say them to the class. The class has to guess which emotion is being conveyed.
2. Say each utterance in different ways (e.g., angrily, sadly, or excitedly), and have the students number each utterance 1, 2, or 3.
3. Write the utterances on the board, say an adjective as a prompt, and have the students, either as individuals or in groups, say the utterances in the appropriate manner.

Contributor

Dominic Cogan is a Lecturer in English at Fukui Prefectural University, Japan. Previously, he has worked in TESOL in Ireland, Ghana, and Oman.

Watch Your Language

Levels
Low intermediate +

Aims
Become more aware of different registers of English

Class Time
20–45 minutes

Preparation Time
20 minutes +

Resources
Some short, taped excerpts of different social situations either recorded by the teacher or adapted from commercially produced work

This activity shows students that the kind of English they use or will hear is often determined by the different roles of the speaker and/or the situation. Using formal or "school" English may cause a strain in social situations among friends whereas using an informal style might be entirely inappropriate in dealing with social superiors such as one's boss.

Procedure

1. Make a recording, authentic or otherwise, of the following types of situations: a judge passing sentence, two young people introducing each other at a party, a new executive being introduced to the board of directors of a large company, a doctor interviewing a patient, a clergyman officiating at a wedding, and two friends talking about their holidays.
2. Distribute to the students a table similar to the one below.

Location	Speaker(s)	Situation
court room	*judge*	*passing sentence*

3. Check that the students understand the headings.
4. Play the tape through. Ask the Students to identify orally the location for each extract. Encourage them to consider what information or clues helped them to identify the locations.

5. Play the tape through again. Have students write in the appropriate location, speaker, and situation on the table. Play each extract separately and allow students time to write on the table.
6. Organize the class into small groups or pairs and ask them to compare their answers.
7. Elicit from the class what their findings were. Introduce the distinction between formal and informal English. With more advanced classes you must discuss the concept of scientific, religious, or legal registers.

Caveats and Options

As a follow-up activity, give students another table listing specific locations, speakers and situations. Have them identify which type of English would be most appropriate and then produce a short role play using the information on the table.

Contributor

Dominic Cogan is a Lecturer in English at Fukui Prefectural University, Japan. Previously, he worked in TESOL in Ireland, Ghana, and Oman.

Tic Tac Toe for Listening

Levels
Beginning +

Aims
Listen to and discriminate between -teen and -ty (e.g., 13 vs. 30)
Learn to ask a student to repeat when the listener does not understand something

Class Time
10–15 minutes

Preparation Time
10–15 minutes

Resources
Five small pieces of paper of one color and five of another color for each student

The distinction between *-ty* and *-teen* is a very difficult listening problem for ESOL students. This kind of listening activity allows for a great deal of listening practice in an enjoyable way.

Procedure

1. If colored paper is not available, use small pieces of paper on which the students' names have been written.
2. Divide the students into pairs.
3. Give each student five small pieces of paper of one color and five of another color. Students should have the same colors as their partners, but colors can vary from pair to pair.
4. Have students draw a big tic tac toe grid on a sheet of paper. The nine squares in the grid should be larger than the small colored pieces of paper.
5. On the board, demonstrate how tic tac toe is played, but instead of using X and O, use colored squares (e.g., with pens on a whiteboard). Draw a large tic tac toe grid so that everyone can easily see it. Number the squares in any order with any 9 of these numbers: 13, 30, 14, 40, 15, 50, 16, 60, 17, 70, 18, 80, 19, 90. Write the number in the top portion of each square.
6. Have two students play the game from their seats. Choose students in different parts of the room. If you have a red and a blue pen, let one of them be red and the other blue. Decide who will go first. Then turn your back to the class and let the first student choose a number. The first student, who is red, says "13" so you should put a small red mark (circle, square, face), in the square with 13. Then the second player, who is blue, calls out a number and you should put a blue mark by that number. Continue until someone has three papers of

the same color in a row or there are no more spaces. If a student calls out "40" (in trying to say "14") but there is no 40 or if 40 has already been filled in, that students loses a turn. In the next game, the student who did not go first goes first.

7. Have students play the game in pairs. They should fill in their grids together so that, the two papers are identical. Have each pair play three games. (Using markers instead of letting students write directly on their grids allows students to play this game several times.)

Caveats and Options

Have pairs exchange papers with other pairs so that they have to play the game again but with numbers that they themselves have not chosen.

Contributor

Keith S. Folse is the author of several ESL texts published by the University of Michigan Press.

Linking Races

Levels
Beginning +

Aims
Develop awareness of
how words are linked
together in normal
speech

Class Time
15–30 minutes

Preparation Time
20 minutes

Resources
Short video clip (1–2
minutes) using linked
speech
Copies of the transcript
of the clip for each
student

Often problems with listening occur not because learners do not know the words said but because they do not *recognize* them in linked speech. Although it may not be necessary for students to be able to produce linked speech, it is important for them to be able to decipher it when they hear it.

Procedure

1. Remind the students that, in natural speech, words are often linked together rather than clearly enunciated.
2. Play the clip once or twice, and have students talk briefly with partners about what they saw and heard. (You may want to do some prelistening exercise to activate schema.)
3. Hand out the transcript of the clip, and have students read through it. Answer any questions they have about it.
4. Have students listen to the video clip and mark words that are linked together.
5. After the students have marked most of the linking on their transcripts, have them practice reading the transcripts, linking words wherever marked. As they get better at producing the linked words, have them read it as quickly as they can.
6. Have the students race against the video clip. Give points to any student who can finish reading faster than the actor or actress in the clip.

Caveats and Options

Before showing the video clip, tell students about some of the ways words are linked together. Give them the transcript and have them go through the script and guess where the linkings are on the video clip.

Contributor

Kenny Harsch, Director of English Education at Kobe YMCA College, Japan, is interested in learner autonomy, student-centered curriculum development, and helping students develop curiosity through inquiry.

Stressed Out

Levels
Beginning–intermediate

Aims
Listen for stressed
words and predict what
information might
follow

Class Time
15–20 minutes

Preparation Time
10 minutes

Resources
Sentences with one
word stressed

Students need to learn that stress can convey meaning and that understanding what they hear in this way can help them predict what they will hear next.

Procedure

1. Write several pairs of sentences. In the first sentence in each pair, one word should be stressed; make sure that the stressed word gives the listener an indication of what the speaker might say next. The second sentence in each pair should come close to confirming the listener's expectation. (See Appendix.)
2. Explain that stress can help listeners predict meaning. Read aloud the first sentence of a pair and ask your students to predict what the speaker might say in the next sentence. Students don't have to get the exact words, but encourage them to give reasons for their predictions.
3. Read the second sentence aloud. Discuss any differences between what the students expected to hear and what they actually heard.
4. Repeat with the remaining pairs of sentences.

Caveats and Options

Record the sentences on tape. The advantage of doing this is that the stressed words will sound identical each time your students hear them.

Appendix: Sample Sentences

Italicized words indicate extra stress

1. John isn't coming on *Thursday*.

(The listener expects to hear that John is coming on another day.) He's coming on *Friday*.

137

2. Alice? She doesn't drive *slowly*!

(The listener expects to hear that Alice drives fast.) She drives *extremely fast*.

3. The *food* is very good at the new restaurant.

(The listener expects to hear that something else at the restaurant isn't very good.) But the *service* is rather slow, and it's *pretty expensive*.

Contributor

Jonathan Hull is a doctoral candidate at the University of Bristol, United Kingdom. He has taught ESOL in Europe, the Mideast, East Asia, and the Pacific. He is one of the coauthors (under Jack C. Richards) of Interchange *(Cambridge University Press).*

Can He or Can't He?

Levels
Any

Aims
Develop skills in understanding negative and affirmative sentences

Class Time
10 minutes

Preparation Time
5 minutes

Resources
Five or six sentences containing *can* or *can't*

To understand differences between negative and affirmative sentences, students need to be aware of differences in vowel length and sentence stress. For example, in the sentence *He can type* the vowel in the word *can* is reduced and unstressed in natural speech, whereas in the sentence *He can't type* the vowel in the word *can't* is lengthened and stressed.

Procedure

1. Write the words *can* and *can't* on the board
2. Say the two sentences below and ask the students if the sentences contained *can* or *can't*.

   He can go to the party tomorrow.
   He can't play basketball.

3. Explain to the students that there are important differences in pronunciation—stress and vowel length—that distinguish the two words.
4. Read each sentence at natural speed and ask students to note down if the sentence contains *can* or *can't*.

Caveats and Options

1. The sentences can either be read (at natural speed) or prerecorded.
2. As a follow-up, have students work in pairs; one person saying the sentences and the other identifying the *can* or *can't*.
3. Find a short sample of recorded natural speech that contains a few examples of *can* and *can't*. Ask students to identify what the speakers can or cannot do.

Contributor

Charles Lockhart is Coauthor, with Jack C. Richards, of Reflective Teaching in the Second Language Classroom *(Cambridge University Press). Pamela Rogerson-Revell is Coauthor, with G. Gilbert, of* Speaking Clearly *(Cambridge University Press).*

Language Lab Karaoke

Levels
Intermediate

Aims
Practice prosodic
features of rhythm,
stress, and intonation

Class Time
30–40 minutes

Preparation Time
20–30 minutes

Resources
Language laboratory
with a master console
Audiotape of a pop
song
Blank audiotape for
each student

Rhythm and intonation patterns in English can be difficult for students to master, particularly if their L1 is tonal, such as Mandarin, and Japanese, and not stress timed. Singing popular songs along with the original singers can give enjoyable and useful practice in the use of prosodic features. The selection of songs is important. Choose pop songs that have natural intonation patterns and clear, accessible lyrics, such as those sung by Elton John, and Whitney Houston.

Procedure

1. Seat students in a language lab, each with a blank audio tape in their booth's cassette player.
2. Hand out the lyrics of a pop song with random words omitted from it.
3. Play the pop song to the whole class and ask them to listen and try to fill in the gaps in their lyric sheets.
4. Ask students to check their lyric sheets in pairs. Elicit the missing words from the class.
5. Play the song again and ask the class to sing along with it. Take the lead in singing, lowering your voice as the class grows in confidence.
6. When the song has finished, ask students to put on their headsets. Tell them that they are going to hear and record the song and that they are going to sing along with it and record their own voices over the original singer's voice. (Note: the students must be able to hear their voice louder than the singers, otherwise they will produce a very distorted rendering of the song.)
7. Play the song again and allow students to record themselves singing over the original song.

8. Ask students to listen to their recording. They will hear their voices foregrounded against the original singer who will be heard "in the background."
9. Play the song a second time and allow students to have a second chance to record their own singing over the voice of the original singer. Once more, ask them to listen to their recording.

Caveats and Options

1. After the two recordings of the student singing along with the original singer ask them to make an unaccompanied recording of themselves singing the song.
2. After the two recordings, ask students to make an unaccompanied spoken recording of the lyrics and then listen to it. Ask them to underline all stressed words. Listen in from the master consul and interrupt when necessary to give feedback.

Contributor

Dino Mahoney has lived and taught in Europe, the Middle East, and the Far East. He was Director of Studies for the British Council in Dubai and Hong Kong.

Listening to Accents

Levels
Intermediate +

Aims
Become sensitive to
different accents in
English

Class Time
30 minutes–1 hour

Preparation Time
Varies

Resources
Tape recorder
Access to a variety of
English speakers

Foreign language students often perform well in class but have difficulty communicating with English speakers outside, quite often because they cannot understand the speaker's accent.

Procedure

1. Make a recording of a variety of English speakers—American, Australian, Indian, Scottish, and others. Have the speakers repeat the same sentence onto the tape first, then ask them to have a short discussion with lots of turn taking.
2. In a multilingual class, have the students describe the different ways people in their country speak their language. Get them to explain which accents they like, which they don't like, and why.
3. Ask students to write on a piece of paper:

   Speaker 1:
   Speaker 2:
   Speaker 3:

   and so forth.

4. Play the tape and ask the students to guess where the speaker comes from (you may want to write up a number of countries on the board to help low-level students).
5. Listen to the tape again and check the answers. Try to get the students to explain how the speakers sound different from each other.
6. Give the students a transcript of the discussion. Tell students to listen to the people talking and mark above the transcript the number of the speaker.
7. Ask students to check their answers with a partner before playing the tape again.

Caveats and Options

As a follow-up speaking exercise the students can try to imitate the accent they like the most. Either in small groups with each group having their own tape recorder and a recording of the tape, or in a language laboratory.

Contributor

Lindsay Miller is a Lecturer in the English Department of the City University of Hong Kong. He has taught EFL in Europe, the Middle East, and Southeast Asia.

Whispers

Levels
Any

Aims
Listen for sound
discrimination
Guess what is heard

Class Time
5–10 minutes

Preparation Time
Minimal

Resources
None

People often have to guess what another person has said. The noises of a busy street or in the subway or the speaker's soft voice may prevent full comprehension. This activity gives the students practice in making guesses about what was said and in listening for sound discrimination.

Procedure

1. Arrange the students into rows of 8–10 students.
2. Whisper a word, phrase, or sentence to the first person in the row.
3. That person whispers whatever was heard to the next person and so on until the message reached the last person in the row.
4. When the message reaches the last person, have that student say the message out loud so that everyone can check whether the message got through.

Caveats and Options

1. Start this activity from either end of the row.
2. Have several messages relayed at once.
3. Start the same message in the middle of the row and see if both ends get the same message.
4. This activity is very useful for practicing sound discrimination. (e.g., /p/ /b/, /v/ /w/)

Contributor

Lindsay Miller is a Lecturer in the English Department at the City University of Hong Kong. He has taught EFL in Europe, the Middle East, and Southeast Asia.

Concertina

Levels
Intermediate +

Aims
Listen for and see the
relationship between
written and spoken
English: pronunciation,
contraction, elision,
assimilation, and
sentence stress

Class Time
30 minutes

Preparation Time
30 minutes

Resources
One long sentence per
group, cut up into
individual words

Employing physical response is a helpful direct strategy that aids some students in their learning.

Procedure

1. Arrange the students into groups. Appoint a spokesperson for the group. Give each individual in the group a word from the sentence (it is a good idea to have extra adjectives on hand so that you can use them or leave them out depending on the size of the group). Do not give the spokesperson a word; tell her to help organize the group and be prepared to say the sentence.
2. Tell the students to work together to think of several sentences that they can make using all the words they have. Once the students have thought of their sentences, ask them to think about the way in which the sentence is spoken.
3. Ask the groups to come to the front of the class in turn. The spokesperson says a sentence to the class, then the group strikes a pose to represent this sentence. Each person represents a word in the sentence: Stressed words stand slightly forward, unstressed words bob down, linked words hold hands, words that completely disappear stand to the side. Tell the spokesperson to say the sentence again and ask the class if they agree that the correct pose has been struck.
4. Engage the class in discussing other ways in which the sentence can be said and ask the group in front to respond to the new suggestions by physically changing their positions.

Caveats and Options

Instead of a spokesperson have the members of the group say their words aloud in turn. They then have to try and say the sentence quickly so that it sounds right.

Contributor

Elizabeth A. Price is a freelance ESOL teacher. She lives in Edinburgh, Scotland.

Spelling Test

Levels
Any

Aims
Reinforce the relationship between spelling and sound

Class Time
10 minutes

Preparation Time
Minimal

Resources
About 10 recently encountered words that have unusual spelling

In this activity students become aware of the unusual spelling of some words in English and associate the spelling with the sound.

Procedure

1. Write a list of the words you wish to test on the board. Ask the students to copy the list down on the right-hand side of a piece of paper as you say them. That is, they have to listen, look, and copy the word.
2. After the students have copied the list of words, clean the board.
3. Tell the students to fold their paper over so that they cannot see the list. Then dictate the list of words again.
4. After you have completed the dictation, allow the students to look at the original list and check their spelling.

Caveats and Options

You can do this activity more than once with the same list of words by changing the order that you dictate them. Simply ask the students to continue folding over their paper so that they can not see the original list.

Contributor

Elizabeth A. Price is a freelance ESOL teacher. She lives in Edinburgh, Scotland.

Learning English With Maps

Levels
Beginning–intermediate

Aims
Practice scanning
Practice recognition of
capitalization and
spelling
Practice the
pronunciation of local
place names
Disciminate between
how the word is said
the local language and
how it is said in English

Class Time
30 minutes +

Preparation Time
5 minutes

Resources
Copies of an English-
language map of a
major city, country, or
area known to students

Scanning English language maps of a known city builds on students' schema of known information and instruct in English grammar, reading strategies, and listening to the accents of native speakers.

Procedure

1. Give one map to each student.
2. Point out and pronounce the place names of importance.
3. Have students repeat the place names as they note their location.
4. In pairs, have students practice pronouncing the names to each other while you monitor.
5. Divide the class into two teams and ask questions about various sites. For example,

   a. In what district is the Tokyo Tower?
   b. Where is the Yamanote train line?
   c. On what street is our school?
   d. What is the name of the largest park?
   e. What is the major shopping district?
   f. Where is the most famous temple?
   g. Where is the Diet building?

6. Award teams points as members respond correctly to your questions. The team with the most points at a certain time wins the game.
7. Have students dictate place names to each other to practice spelling and checking.

Caveats and Options

1. Have students bring English-language maps of places they are interested in.

2. For testing or very large classes, write down the questions.
3. As students prepare for arrival at a U.S. location, use maps of that city or campus.

Contributors

Devi Spencer teaches at the University of Houston, Texas. Wynell Biles teaches at Texas A & M University, College Station, Texas, in the United States.

Listening for Differences in Meaning

Levels
Low intermediate

Aims
Understand different meanings determined by the placement of stress between adjective-noun phrases and adjective-noun compounds

Class Time
10 minutes

Preparation Time
20 minutes

Resources
Any adjective-noun phrases and adjective-noun compounds that illustrate differences in meaning conveyed through stress patterns Visual aids such as drawings or pictures to check students' comprehension (See Appendix)

It is very difficult for nonnative speakers, especially those whose L1s are syllable-timed languages such as Japanese, to understand the role that stress plays in assigning meaning. Avery and Ehrlich (1992) discuss the differences in stress patterns between adjective-noun phrases and adjective-noun compounds. For example:

That's a black board (a board that is black).
That's a chalkboard (a board for writing on—green or black).

In the first example, which contains the adjective-noun phrase, the noun *board* receives major stress whereas the adjective *black* receives minor stress. In the second example, the adjective-noun compound, major and minor stress fall on *black* and *board* respectively. Avery and Ehrlich state that "it is beneficial to have students distinguish between phrases and compounds on the basis of stress" (p. 69).

Procedure

1. Present the students with two sentences that contain an adjective-noun phrase and an adjective-noun compound respectively.
2. Present the students with two pictures that illustrate the differences in meaning reflected in the sentences.
3. Explain to the students that the meaning of sentences can differ depending on whether major stress falls on either adjective or noun.
4. Put the drawings on the chalkboard or project the transparency on which the pictures are drawn.
5. Read out the sentences and ask the students to identify which drawings best describe the meaning of the sentences.

Caveats and Options

Do this activity as an oral exercise. First, show the picture to the students. Then have them produce sentences with correct stress patterns that correspond to the pictures.

References and Further Reading

Avery, P., & Ehrlich, S. (1992). *Teaching American English pronunciation*. Oxford: Oxford University Press.

Appendix: Sample Compounds

Sentences to be read by the teacher:

1. He saw a moving van. He saw a moving van.
2. They work in a green house. They work in a greenhouse.
3. I saw a black bird. I saw a blackbird.
4. He goes to the white house. He goes to the White House.
5. He has been in that dark room of his since this morning. He has been in that darkroom of his since this morning.

Contributor

Hiroyuki Umeno is a graduate student in the TESOL program at Temple University, Japan, in Tokyo.

◆ Listening and Vocabulary
Teaching New Vocabulary Through Listening Comprehension

Levels
Any

Aims
Help students hear new words in context
Encourage students to make logical guesses as to orthography and meaning

Class Time
20–30 minutes

Preparation Time
20 minutes

Resources
Listening passage containing new words, preferably from the same lexical set (e.g., Disaster, see References and Further Reading)

Especially if done in a language laboratory, this task provides ample extensive and intensive listening practice and encourages students to use context to guess the meaning of new words and to apply any rules of spelling they are familiar with.

Procedure

1. Write enough true/false questions to lead students to an understanding of the gist of the listening passage.
2. Delete around eight new words from the tapescript. Make a photocopy of the questions and doctored tapescript (back-to-back) for each student.
3. Tell the students to listen to the passage and answer as many true/false questions as possible without looking at the tapescript.
4. Tell the students to check their answers by listening and reading the tapescript simultaneously.
5. Ask the students to complete the gaps in the tapescript by listening intensively to the new words.
6. Check the answers, correct spelling mistakes, and check that the correct meaning of the words has been guessed from the context.

Caveats and Options

As a follow-up give a short dictation the following lesson that incorporates the new vocabulary, or ask students to work in pairs to correct any mistakes made in the dictation. This can be done by first one students reading out their dictation passage while the other listens for errors, then change around.

References and Further Reading

Bell, J. (1989). *Soundings.* Harlow, England: Longman.

Contributor

William Bickerdike is Senior Teacher at the British Council, Riyadh, Saudi Arabia.

Listening Comprehension Through Pictures

Levels
Beginning; children

Aims
Assess knowledge of vocabulary concepts at the preproduction stage Demonstrate an understanding of the vocabulary by performing the required actions

Class Time
15 minutes

Preparation Time
10 minutes

Resources
Reproducible picture Crayons or markers

Caveats and Options

Contributor

Children can demonstrate their knowledge of the target vocabulary through the use of physical responses, lowering their stress level in trying to use a new language.

Procedure

1. Photocopy enough copies of the picture to give one to each child. Give each child a copy of the picture and crayons or markers.
2. Give directions using the target vocabulary. This vocabulary should include the set of words related to objects in the picture plus another set of words used for directions. The following is an example:

   Draw a Halloween picture with pumpkins, a witch, cats, a fence, and other symbols of the holiday. (Pause between each item to give the child enough time to think about what they will draw, and then draw it.)

3. If the target vocabulary is color words, say, "Color the witch's hat green. Color the pumpkin blue. Color the fence pink. Use colors the child will not immediately associate with the object, such as green for a witch's hat, so that they process the information and show that they understand the name of the color. If the target vocabulary consists of prepositions instruct the children, "Draw a line under the witch. Draw a circle around the cat."

Once the children have the idea of listening to and following instructions related to the picture, pair them up and ask them to give each other instructions.

Judi Braverman is an ESOL teacher at Lindell School in Long Beach, New York, in the United States. She has trained ESOL student teachers from Hofstra and Adelphi Universities.

The Complete Person

Levels
Beginning +

Aims
Follow the description
of a person

Class Time
5–10 minutes per
description

Preparation Time
None

Resources
Paper and pencil
Chalkboard

Students need to discriminate personal traits. This total physical response activity allows them to respond through information transfer (drawing a picture).

Procedure

1. Draw a figure of a person on the board.
2. Read a brief description of a person and ask the students to complete the person. A wide variety of vocabulary and structures could be used, for example,

   Mary is a very beautiful young lady. She's about 20 years old. She's not very tall. She has curly blonde hair and big, blue eyes. Right now she's wearing a green striped blouse and a purple skirt. She doesn't wear glasses . . .

   By mixing in negatives, progressives, and other structures, the teacher can check comprehension of stressed and unstressed speech (e.g., *can/can't*) and vocabulary control.
3. Have students compare drawings and discuss the differences. This can lead to functional practice in asking/clarifying/correcting information.

Caveats and Options

1. You may wish to review pertinent vocabulary or write down two or three short descriptions before class.
2. Use the activity as a student-to-student dictation (with a drawing on the board or as pair work) for pronunciation (aural/oral discrimination of words such as *short/shirt*).
3. Use the activity on the reading part of a test, especially in a functional unit about describing people.
4. Higher level classes could be given a diagram of an empty room.

Contributor

Dennis Bricault teaches at North Park College, Chicago, Illinois, in the United States.

Finding an Apartment

Levels
Beginning

Aims
Consolidate vocabulary already introduced in a contextualized way

Class Time
10 minutes

Preparation Time
20 minutes

Resources
Audiotaped conversation of one person showing an apartment to a prospective tenant
List of words

Students are often taught new vocabulary in a decontextualized way. This activity uses the vocabulary that has already been introduced in a way that illustrates how the words can be used.

Procedure

1. Explain to students that they are going to hear a conversation between a landlord and a prospective tenant.
2. Give out a list of words to the students and explain that they should listen to the conversation and circle the nouns on the list that they hear. Do the first noun together as an example.
3. Play the tape without pausing.
4. Tell the students that they will hear the tape again and that this time they should circle the adjectives they hear (again do an example first).
5. Play the tape a second time.
6. Tell the students to listen once more to the tape, this time drawing a line between the appropriate noun and its corresponding adjective as heard on the tape:

kitchen	large
lounge	beautiful
window	modern
cooker	small
dining room	pretty
carpet	expensive
bathroom	old
bed	new
heater	convenient

Caveats and Options

Have students listen to the tape again and number each noun phrase in the order they hear them.

Contributor

Dominic Cogan is a Lecturer in English at Fukui Prefectural University, Japan. Previously, he taught ESOL in Ireland, Ghana, and Oman.

TV Commercials

Levels
Intermediate

Aims
Listen for drivel

Class Time
30–45 minutes

Preparation Time
15 minutes

Resources
Several taped TV
commercials that
contain few direct
statements of fact and
lots of unsubstantiated
claims

Students should be able to identify the language of advertising and distinguish between it and factual statements.

Procedure

1. Introduce a prelistening task about advertisements on TV. Which ones do the students like? Which don't they like? Why?
2. Tell the class that they are going to watch some advertisements. While they are viewing they should try to complete the following table:

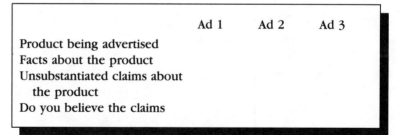

	Ad 1	Ad 2	Ad 3
Product being advertised			
Facts about the product			
Unsubstantiated claims about the product			
Do you believe the claims			

3. After each advertisement, give the students a few minutes to complete the table. After viewing all the advertisements, arrange the students into groups and let them discuss the information in their tables.
4. Play the advertisements again. This time the students should note the vocabulary and/or grammatical structures being used to make statements of fact, and make claims.
5. Elicit the vocabulary/grammatical structures from the students. Discuss how they are used to enhance particular products.

Caveats and Options

As a follow-up exercise, ask the students to produce their own advertisements and present them to the class.

Contributor

David Gardner teaches ESP in the English Centre of the University of Hong Kong. He has taught in secondary, technical, and tertiary institutions in a number of countries.

What's This Film About?

Levels
High intermediate +

Aims
Understand vocabulary
through
contextualization

Class Time
40 minutes

Preparation Time
10–15 minutes

Resources
A feature film
Video tape player

Students should learn that they can help themselves understand new lexis or unfamiliar structure by looking at the context in which it occurs.

Procedure

1. From the first 5 minutes of the film, select 10 items that will challenge the students. The items could be words, phrases, grammatical structures, or a mixture.
2. Play the first 5 minutes of the film with the sound only (cover the monitor screen with a cloth). Have students try to define the items.
3. Have students in groups try to refine their definitions.
4. Play the film again, this time with the sound and image.
5. Have the class discuss definitions.
6. Play the film again to illustrate points where necessary.
7. Ask students what they think the film is about.
8. Give a brief synopsis of the film.

Caveats and Options

1. Do not give a synopsis but tell students where they can view the film.
2. Ask students to report back after viewing the film: Who were the main characters? What was the story? How did it end?
3. This activity works particularly well in areas where English language films are shown on TV. In such circumstances, rent a film that you will show later in the week.

Contributor

David Gardner teaches ESP in the English Centre of the University of Hong Kong. He has taught in secondary, technical, and tertiary institutions in a number of countries.

Crossword Listening

Levels
Any

Aims
Focus on descriptions
and definitions

Class Time
20–30 minutes

Preparation Time
Varies

Resources
Specially prepared
crossword with no clues
or words, only the
blank spaces
Audiotape of
descriptions of the
words to be filled in on
the crossword

Learners need to be able to describe well, and for tertiary students description is an essential skill.

Procedure

1. Prepare, in advance, the crossword you wish to use. Include vocabulary your students have only just learned or specific vocabulary if you teach in an ESP situation.
2. Hand out the crossword and discuss the topic of crosswords for a few minutes. Do your students like them? Do they do them in their own language? Have they ever tried to do one in a foreign language before? Make sure that the students realize that once they have a few of the words, some of the filled-in letters will help them with subsequent words.
3. Tell the students that they are going to listen to descriptions of the words from a tape. Play the descriptions one at a time, and allow the students time to think about the word before playing the next description. The descriptions can build up from vague information to specific information giving the students more clues with each sentence. Pause at each stage to give them time to think and see how much information they need before they know the word. For example, one across:

   Well, part of it is round (pause), although you can find square or other shaped ones (pause). There are some moving parts on it (pause), and it has a strap (pause). It can be made from metal or plastic (pause). It's quite small (pause). It has marks, or numbers on it (pause). We say that it has a face and hands (pause), but it's inanimate.
   Answer: A watch

4. After the students have listened to all the descriptions, have them compare their answers with a partner before checking with you.

Caveats and Options

There are many possible variations to this crossword activity. Give half the students all the Down words, and the other half all the Across words in the crossword. Or pair the students up and tell them to give each other descriptions/definitions of the words so that they can complete the crossword.

References and Further Reading

See Miller, L. (1992). Using games in an EST class. *TESOL Journal, 2,* 38-39, for more information on paired crosswords.

Contributor

Lindsay Miller is a Lecturer in the English Department of the City University of Hong Kong. He has taught EFL in Europe, the Middle East, and Southeast Asia.

. . . And First, the News Headlines

Levels
Low intermediate +

Aims
Develop skills in
decoding several
language aspects

Class Time
20 minutes (advanced)
45 minutes
(intermediate)

Preparation Time
15–20 minutes

Resources
Taped headlines from a
recent international
radio news broadcast,
such as BBC World
Service

Headlines typically comprise four short sentences rich in the present tenses, reported speech, articles, and descriptors and are usually free from slang and idiom. Students enjoy working with them because students at lower levels often feel confined by coursebook material and isolated from international events by their limited language ability.

Procedure

1. Listen to the tape before class. Put blanks on the board to represent every word. Write in words that are outside students' vocabulary range or are irrelevant to your lesson.
2. Tell the class that all gapped words are within their vocabulary range. Play the tape to the class once or twice. Then play it clause by clause as students write what they hear (allow time for thinking and writing). Repeat until two or three students have finished or no further progress is being made.
3. Invite one student to fill in the gaps on the board as other students call out words. This produces lots of valuable discussion; stay silent unless the final choice is wrong.
4. Make a game of filling in the remaining gaps, either by playing Hangman or giving clues.
5. Play the tape again to reinforce the listening skill.

For example,

The Bosnian Serbs have continued the assault on the capital, Sarajevo, during a third night of fighting.
   (present perfect, stress, different sounds of *the*, similar sounds of *have ('ve)* and *of*, prepositions)

The United States is considering sanctions against China, which, it believes, has exported sensitive missile technology to Pakistan.
(present perfect and continuous, relative clauses and pronouns, prepositions)

Contributor

David Pepperle is a teacher at Seafield School of English, Christchurch, New Zealand.

What's the Clue?

Levels
Low intermediate

Aims
Develop skill in
detecting the meaning
of new words in a
listening activity

Class Time
20–30 minutes

Preparation Time
20–25 minutes

Resources
Short story or a news
article, a few unfamiliar
words

Students can develop the ability to guess meanings of new words by listening for clues from the context in which these words occur.

Procedure

1. Remind students that they can understand a text better by listening for clues to words they don't know.
2. Prepare them for the text with a prelistening activity: Read a sentence with a new word, and ask what clues they heard to help guess the word's meaning.
3. Repeat Step 2 if necessary.
4. Ask students to listen while you read the text for the first time.
5. Let them write down any new words they hear as you reread the text. Allow a brief time after this reading so they can write meanings beside each word.
6. Discuss new words they found and how they used clues in the story to guess meanings.

Caveats and Options

1. Tape the text.
2. More advanced students may not need to listen to the text a second time.

Contributor

Carol Potter has an MEd in TESOL and teaches at Temple University, Japan.

Green Velveteen Pantaloons

Levels
Beginning

Aims
Recycle clothes
vocabulary

Class Time
A few minutes

Preparation Time
None

Resources
None

Recycling vocabulary is important especially with students at lower language levels. Teachers need to try and find different ways to do this without boring their students.

Procedure

1. Involve the students in an activity that requires a class feedback session.
2. While the students are involved in their activity, walk around the class and monitor what they are wearing.
3. At the feedback session, instead of naming the student to answer the question, say "Would someone who is wearing a blue skirt/a striped . . . checked . . . spotted shirt/brown brogues/trainers etc. Answer this question."
4. The students should be able to identify whomever you are describing. Some of the vocabulary can be new and reviewed at the end of the lesson. Remember not to look at the student you want the answer from.

Contributor

Elizabeth A. Price is a freelance ESOL teacher. She lives in Edinburgh, Scotland.

Santa's Dimples

Levels
Beginning; young
learners

Aims
Listen to a poem and
comprehend a
description

Class Time
55 minutes

Preparation Time
10–15 minutes

Resources
Copy of *The Night
Before Christmas*
Index cards

Students listen to the American favorite *The Night Before Christmas* and demonstrate their understanding of the poem by drawing a picture of Santa Claus. Emphasis is on the vocabulary describing Santa.

Procedure

1. Prior to class, make up index cards showing the following words:

dimples	back	face
eyes	head	beard
cheeks	foot	wink
belly	nose	mouth
pipe	chin	teeth

2. Read the book *The Night Before Christmas* aloud.
3. Reread the section describing Santa and ask the students to draw picture of what they hear.
4. Compare pictures and discuss.
5. Hold up an index card, call out the word, and have the student point to the body part.

Caveats and Options

This lesson works well after you have taught some body parts. It was used successfully to put a group of middle school learners in the Christmas spirit.

Contributor

Sharon Sealy, ABD, is currently researching academic competence in mainstream classrooms at the University of Georgia, in the United States. Her interests include multicultural awareness and the Hispanic culture.

Part III: Listening to Authentic Material

Creating Listening Expectation

Levels
High
beginning–intermediate

Aims
Focus on listening for
expected words using
authentic materials

Class Time
15–20 minutes

Preparation Time
30 minutes

Resources
Any authentic listening
material a little beyond
the level of the students

Students should be allowed to listen to material that is authentic, of interest to them, and of which they are aware. When students know what to listen for, they are able to perceive and understand material better (Ur, 1987).

Procedure

1. Find an appropriate text with a topic students are interested in or aware of.
2. Prepare to read or play the text at normal speed.
3. Locate text words that can be determined either grammatically or contextually.
4. Delete these words, making a clozed text.
5. Introduce the topic or the text to students and create schema.
6. Give the cloze activity to the students.
7. Ask students to read through the cloze text.
8. On the board, list the words students suggest for each blank.
9. Read or play the text, having students confirm or correct their expectations.
10. Return to the list on the board and note which of their guesses were appropriate.

Caveats and Options

1. Use a listening textbook, pausing occasionally for students to suggest possible words.
2. Give students a choice of words to consider for each cloze blank.

References and Further Reading

Ur, P. (1987). *Teaching listening comprehension.* Cambridge: Cambridge University Press.

Contributor

Gail Beran is a teacher at Tokyo YMCA College in Japan.

Details, Please

Levels
High intermediate +

Aims
Improve listening
accuracy

Class Time
25–30 minutes

Preparation Time
10–15 minutes

Resources
Audiotaped radio
interview, talk show or
feature program about 5
minutes long

It is challenging for learners to try to follow a native speaker's speech, and depending on the degree of success, this activity can be a highly motivating.

Procedure

1. Explain to the students that they are going to listen to native speakers. Tell the students the type of program they will listen to but nothing about the topic or speakers.
2. Play the tape once through for general comprehension. Elicit the main points of the conversation. Rewind the tape.
3. Play the conversation again, this time in sections. Pause the tape and ask the students to transcribe as much as they can of the section they just heard.
4. Arrange the students into pairs or small groups. Ask them to try to reconstruct the conversation using all their transcriptions.
5. Once the pairs or groups have made an attempt to reconstruct the conversation, play the tape once more for them to check their dialogues.

Caveats and Options

1. Choose parts of a radio program that has speakers with different accents. Discuss which accent is easier to understand for your students and why.
2. As a follow-up, have students record the dialogue, listen to their own version of the same conversation, and compare the original with their production.

Contributor

Erlinda R. Boyle is Senior Instructor at the English Language Teaching Unit of the Chinese University of Hong Kong.

Weather Report

Levels
Beginning

Aims
Listen for specific details
Listen for numbers 1–99

Class Time
5–10 minutes

Preparation Time
Varies

Resources
Weather broadcast
taped from the radio (or
TV, if possible)
Cassette player (or VCR)
Local map
Names of cities from the
report on index cards

Students at the beginning level tend to "shut off" when faced with rapid, natural speech. This activity shows them that, with a limited knowledge of a new language, they are able to accomplish a task by knowing what to listen for.

Procedure

1. Demonstrate how students should not try to approach the listening: Playing the weather report without any preparation and asking random questions about temperatures in various cities.
2. Pass out index cards with the names of cities mentioned in the weather report. Play the tape again telling the students to listen to the report again, but only for the temperature of the city on the card.
3. Check comprehension by calling out city names at random and asking students to give the temperature.
4. Write the cities and corresponding temperatures on the board and the class could listen to the report a third time to verify the information.

Caveats and Options

1. Rather than attempt to write down temperatures at first, students can hold up the cards when the cities are mentioned, either as a preteaching activity or during the second playing of the report. Higher level classes can listen for weather conditions (e.g., rain, snow).
2. This activity can be extended to any level for news reports (e.g., recognition of names, cities, topics) and can be made as challenging as you wish.

Contributor

Dennis Bricault teaches at North Park College, Chicago, Illinois, in the United States.

Listen and Ask *- good activity for first group lesson*

Levels
Beginning–intermediate

Aims
Listen attentively to
natural speech

Class Time
5 minutes

Preparation Time
None

Resources
Mounted poster

Interesting content with a communicative purpose is a good stimulus for encouraging students to listen attentively. In this activity, students bring a familiar object to class, tell the class about it, and answer their classmates' questions. A 5-minute daily sharing activity creates a channel for students to talk, to listen, to understand, and to ask about one another. This activity is particularly useful at the beginning of the academic year.

Procedure

1. Model the activity by bringing to class something you would like to talk about, such as shells or a holiday souvenir. Tell the class something about the object (for a beginning class limit the object to three, for higher-level classes ramble on for several minutes). For example, show a low-level class, some shells and tells them that (a) collecting shells is one of your hobbies; (b) you are interested in collecting shells with different shapes, sizes, and colors; and (c) you have collected shells for 5 years. After that, ask one or two questions about what you have said: "How many years have I collected my shells?"
2. Invite the class to prepare three to five *wh*-questions about the object, such as Where did you collect your shells? How many shells do you have? Why do you like collecting shells? Who collects shells with you? Will you give your shells to us? Answer the listeners' questions.
3. Instruct students to think of a favorite or interesting object to bring to class. For each class, choose one or two students as speakers to bring an object (e.g., a poster, a toy, a book, a photo) and talk about it. Ask the speakers to think of something to say about their objects and be prepared to ask the class some *wh*-questions. Encourage them to seek help from you for preparation.

173

4. Invite one speaker to the front of the class to present an object and to ask the class questions (do not worry about accuracy, or pronunciation during the presentation, but make a note of any difficulties and deal with them later). After the presentation, give the class a few minutes to plan their questions, then invite the class to ask the speaker questions.

After finishing the activity, the speaker invites one or two classmates to prepare the next day's Listen and Ask. Then the speaker draws the object and writes his name on a poster.

Caveats and Options

This activity can be carried out at the beginning or the end of the lesson. Have students form small groups (four or five classmates each) to do the activity. You can change the topic to favorite activities, movies, places, or festivals. The group discussion is the basis for an extended informal oral report. The group leader can be responsible to report their discussion to the class. If students have difficulty in asking the speaker questions, make suggestions orally or in writing.

Contributor

Marie Cheung, a former secondary English teacher in Hong Kong, now is a PhD student in the Department of English at City University of Hong Kong.

Listening to TV Soaps

Levels
Any

Class Time
2–3 hours +

Preparation Time
30 minutes–1 hour

Resources
Television

Listening comprehension is a very complex process in both L1 and L2 communication (Dunkel, 1991). This activity is an attempt to make programs, especially soap operas, more accessible to all levels of L2 learners. You should adjust the schema to the proficiency of the students and spend as much time as necessary.

Soaps are useful for teaching listening comprehension for the following reasons:

1. Soaps are shown on a sequential/continuing basis either daily (*General Hospital; Guiding Light*) or weekly (*Dallas; Knots Landing; Falcon Crest*). You can tape daily shows and thus control the pace of showing the material for all levels.
2. Soaps, although not spontaneous in their use of language, offer the closest examples of real communication in a variety of settings.
3. The use of TV soaps outside the classroom will give the learners a few more hours of study and enable them to take a greater responsibility for their own learning.
4. TV soaps usually continue for 5-10 years on TV, unlike commercially produced video programs—a good source of motivation for the L2 learner to apply herself to the task. The procedure follows Morley and Lawrence's (1971) guidelines for using film in the L2 class.

Procedure

1. Fun

    Ask the students to watch the preselected soap drama from beginning to end without having to produce anything. Many students return with high anxiety at not being able to understand the show. Remind them that Stage 1 was designed for the students to get a feeling for the soap.

2. Names and Faces

Ask the students to concentrate on one activity: listening to all the names they hear and writing them down. The next day in class, ask students to compare the names they heard and come up with a group answer. Have class members write a list of names on the board. Remind the students that they should continue to write any new name they hear during the next stages of listening.

3. Relationships

Preteach vocabulary on immediate family relationships and cultural differences concerned with relationships. Put students into groups and have them compare answers. Ask each group to draw a family tree or trees. Discussions can ensue, depending on the level of the students, about culture differences and the family.

4. Personalities

Teach students vocabulary that describes people's personalities. Ask them to write a personality description of each character in the soap opera (they already have the names).

Encourage them to give their personal opinions about the characters. In the next class, have groups compare answers and, if possible, develop a group description. This is not always an easy task because some students have some strong personal feelings about the characters.

5. Summary

Ask students to write all they can about the episode they are watching. This summary can be as detailed as you want or the students are able to produce. Again, have students compare their summaries in groups and develop a group summary.

6. Fun

Many of the more proficient learners may be hooked by this stage and will want to continue to watch the soap for their personal interest. Class discussions can be designed around any topic of interest that the students feel is relevant.

Caveats and Options

1. Pacing through each stage depends on the proficiency level of the group. Beginning students can be exposed to small portions at a time,

in class, and more proficient students can be assigned each stage weekly. Very advanced students could watch the soaps daily.

2. If you are using a comprehension approach (e.g., Postovsky, 1974), you can eliminate discussions and ask for a written response. You can focus on microexercises of language use (e.g., idioms, vocabulary) or macroexercises (e.g., cultural differences and what they entail).

3. You can at any stage of the process have a quiz or a multiple-choice test. However, testing should not be a major focus because each student will be at a different level of listening proficiency.

4. After one cycle, you can transfer this method to a different show.

References and Further Reading

Dunkel, P. (1991). Listening in the native and second/foreign language: Toward an integration of research and practice. *TESOL Quarterly, 25*, 431–457.

Morley, J. M., & Lawrence, M. (1971). The use of films in teaching English as an L2. *Language Learning, 22*, 101–105.

Postovsky, V. (1974). The effects of delay in oral practice at the beginning of L2 learning. *Modern Language Journal, 58*, 229–239.

Contributor

Thomas S. C. Farrell has been living and teaching in Korea for the past 12 years. He is Assistant Professor in the Department of English Language Education, Korea University.

Fast Speech Dictation

Levels
Low intermediate +

Aims
Develop skill at
listening to natural
spoken English

Class Time
1 hour

Preparation Time
10–15 minutes

Resources
10 sentences to be
dictated
Chalkboard

This exercise is designed to help students bridge the gap between written and spoken language in a manner that is both challenging and interactive. All structures and vocabulary should be familiar to the students. The sentences may focus on (a) a particular aspect of fast speech, (b) a grammatical structure, (c) or a function (see Appendix).

Procedure

1. Before class, read through the sentences and underline words that are omitted or altered in reduced speech. Practice saying the sentences so that you will be sure to read them the same way each time you repeat them to the class.
2. Write the sentence numbers on the board. Besides each sentence, write the number of words in that sentence.
3. Divide the students into pairs. Have them sit close enough to see each other's papers.
4. Give the students the following instructions:

   I will dictate 10 sentences to you. I will repeat each sentence as many times as you like, but I will not say the sentences slowly. If you want to hear a sentence again, please call out, "repeat."

   On the board, I have written the number of words in each sentence. When you are satisfied with your sentence, please count the number of words to see if you have the correct number.

   Please work together with your partner. Try to agree on your final sentence.

5. Read Sentence 1 once at normal speed. If this is the first time you have done a fast speech dictation, the students may be a little shocked. Do not repeat the sentence unless requested to do so by a student. If

required, continue repeating the sentence, maybe 10 to 15 times, until all the students seem satisfied. Encourage students to compare and discuss their sentence with the partner.

6. Work through the other sentences in the same manner.

7. When you have finished, ask the students if they would like any of the sentences repeated.

8. Divide the chalkboard into 10 squares and number them.

9. Assign sentences to different pairs. Ask them to come up to the board and write their sentences in the appropriate squares. Have all the pairs do this at the same time. (Be sure to have enough chalk on hand.)

9. Correct the sentences. Underline words or letters that are reduced or omitted in fast speech. Praise students who made educated guesses even though they might have been wrong.

10. To wrap up, erase the board, ask the students to turn over their papers, and read the sentences one final time.

Appendix: Sample Sentences

(Suitable for a low intermediate class)

1. It's nice *to* meet you. (5 words)
2. *What do* you do? (4 words)
3. Where are *you* from? (4 words)
4. *Do you* have any children? (5 words)
5. How long *have you* been *here*? (6 words)
6. Have *you* ever been *to* the U.S.? (7 words)
7. What *do you* like *to* do in *your* free time? (10 words)
8. How long *have you* been *studying* English? (7 words)
9. What *kind of* sports *do you* like? (7 words)
10. *Do you have* any hobbies? (5 words)

Note: Italicized words indicate words whose pronunciation would be altered in fast speech according to the dialect of this writer (from: Seattle, Washington, in the United States).

Contributor

Kelly Fowler is an English instructor at the Japan Intercultural Academy of Municipalities, Otsu City, Japan.

What's in the News?

Levels
Intermediate

Aims
Practice authentic
listening

Class Time
35 minutes

Preparation Time
5 minutes

Resources
Several copies of an
audiotape of a live radio
news broadcast,
preferably a recent one
Several tape recorders

Working with a live broadcast is much more demanding than using edited material. In this activity, all students should listen to the same broadcast.

Procedure

1. Begin with a prelistening task. Ask the students what the main stories were on the news last night. Do not ask for details at this stage, only the headlines.
2. Arrange the students into groups of four and give each group a tape recorder and a tape of the radio news.
3. Tell the class to listen to the news straight through without pausing and try to write down the headlines.
4. Assign each group one of the stories to listen to carefully. Tell the students that they must only listen to the tape once more, after which the group has to produce a summary of the story that they listened to.
5. Ask one member of each group to come up to the front of the class. Tell the speakers to arrange themselves into the order in which they heard the news stories on the radio. The whole class can help if the speakers have a problem here.
6. Have the speakers read through their summaries of the news stories while the rest of the class listens.
7. Play the radio version again and discuss with the class the accuracy of the summaries they heard.

Caveats and Options

Assign this activity as a homework task by asking the students to listen to the news on television the evening before their class and write a summary of one of the main points. In class, group the students according to the stories they listened to and have them produce a summary for presentation to the class.

Contributor

David Gardner teaches ESP in the English Centre of the University of Hong Kong. He has taught secondary, technical, and tertiary institutions in a number of countries.

Listening to the News

Levels
Intermediate +

Aims
Develop skill in
selective listening for
specific information

Class Time
20–30 minutes

Preparation Time
15–20 minutes

Resources
Current videotaped
news broadcast from
radio or TV

The news is an authentic source of the language that is readily available to students, even in an ESOL situation. Listening to the news is a real-life use of the language that can encourage students to practice their language skills outside of class.

Procedure

1. Conduct a class discussion about listening to the news. Possible discussion questions include (a) Do you prefer learning about the news from reading the newspaper, listening to the radio, or watching TV? Why? (b) What types of news items are generally reported on the news (e.g., stories about war, natural disasters, famous people, economics)? (c) What areas of the world have been in the news recently? What has been happening in these places? (d) What news stories do you expect to hear about on today's (or last night's) news?

2. Use students' answers to make two lists on the board: a list of places from Question c and a list of types of news items from Question b.

3. Play the first part of the news (the headlines). Students listen and decide (a) how many news items there are and (b) which of the places on the board the news items are about.

4. Play the rest of the tape. Have students listen and decide which types of news the stories are about (they might be about more than one).

5. Have students discuss which story they are most interested in and why. The class then votes for the news items they would like to listen to again in more detail.

6. Play these items again. Students listen intensely and answer the following questions:

	Item One	Item Two	Item Three
Who is involved?			
What did these people do?			
Where did the event take place?			
Why is this event important?			

Caveats and Options

1. As an extension, ask students to discuss what they think will happen as a result of the event and what historical significance they think the event will have.
2. Have the students do a role play based on one news item they hear, with one student relating the event to a partner. Students might begin their role play as follows:

   A: Hey. Have you heard the news?
   B: No. What happened?

   This role play could be used to practice certain grammatical structures (e.g., present perfect and past tense), or expressions and intonation patterns to express surprise, regret, and other emotions.

Contributor

Charles Lockhart is University Lecturer, City University of Hong Kong, and coauthor (with J. C. Richards) of Reflective Teaching in Second Language Classrooms (Cambridge University Press).

Multilevel Discussion

Levels
Any

Aims
Listen and respond to
near-authentic material

Class Time
20–40 minutes

Preparation Time
Varies

Resources
Tape of a tour itinerary
or vacation commercial
Tape recorder
Chalkboard

Learners need to practice responding to authentic audio- or videotaped materials in language classes. This activity is constructed around a specific topic or task so students can experience a chunk of authentic language both cognitively and affectively. Rogers and Medley (1988) suggest using authentic materials. The vacation commercial used here is adapted from an ESOL book and tape set by Pavlik (1985, p. 90).

Procedure

1. Play the tape. Have learners respond according to their ability in groups if desired. Low-level students can answer the following question:

   The item presented is a (a) weather report (b) sports report (c) travel advertisement

2. Ask intermediate levels to answer the first exercise and the following:

   What activities are available? How can you get to Palm Island? Where do you leave from? How long does it take to get to Palm Island? How much does it cost?

3. Have higher levels answer all of the above as well as the following:

   How do you arrange your trip? Is it a campsite or a full-service resort? Would you like to go? Why? Suggest other activities not listed in the commercial. Write (or make an oral presentation of) a summary of your last trip.

   or

   You are setting up a vacation plan for your class. Try to sell it to them.

them. Tell them that during their presentation they can refer to their notes for ideas but they should try to speak as spontaneously as they can.

5. In addition to the notes, ask students to write four opinion questions that, following their report, they can use for discussion in their group.

6. Tell students the date on which their report is to be given in class. If more convenient, arrange for half of the reports to be presented during one class and the remainder at another time.

7. On the day of the reports, ask the students to form groups with two or three classmates, making sure that everybody in a group has a different topic.

8. Give each student 15 minutes to report and ask their opinion questions.

Caveats and Options

Students who have a VCR can rent documentaries (e.g., *National Geographic*) from video shops.

Contributor

Susan Parks has coordinated ESOL adult education programs at Concordia University and Universite de Montreal, in Canada. She is currently involved in ESOL teacher education.

Strip Story Dictation

Levels
Intermediate

Aims
Improve sentence-level
listening comprehension
Develop understanding
of cohesion and
rhetorical structure of
short passages

Class Time
15–30 minutes

Preparation Time
10–15 minutes

Resources
Short narratives clipped
from newspapers or
magazines or teacher-
written stories

Procedure

1. Select a short article of about 10 or so sentences.
2. Scramble the sentences and number them consecutively in their new order.
3. Put students in groups of three or four.
4. Dictate the numbered sentences to the students at least three times using conversational/lecture rate of speed.
5. Following the third dictation, call for questions on the dictation so that students may ask for repetition of any troublesome items.
6. Have students check their individual work and then, working as a group, come to a consensus as to what the individual sentences are as well as the order in which they should appear. Students should hold their discussions in English if at all possible.
7. When all groups are satisfied with their work, select a group at random to write its story on the chalkboard. Query the other groups to ascertain if they agree. Make only changes suggested by the students, reserving your corrections until the students have exhausted their resources.
8. Make corrections as necessary by first pointing out where the error or errors occur and asking for suggestions as to corrections. If students are unable to make the appropriate correction, provide the correct information.

9. Continue the discussion as to the meaning of the passage, if necessary.

10. As a culminating activity, have the students set their versions aside, erase the chalkboard, and read the unscrambled version to the students to see if they are now able to understand it in its entirety.

Contributor

Ted Plaister is the retired founding chair of the department of English as a Second Language, University of Hawaii, in the United States. He is the author of ESOL Case Studies: The Real World of L2 Teaching and Administration *(Regents Prentice Hall).*

Lyrical Listening

Levels
Beginning

Aims
Practice listening to
native speakers in
context
Build on cultural
knowledge of American
music
Increase vocabulary

Class Time
20–60 minutes

Preparation Time
Minimal

Resources
Radio
Overhead projector
(OHP) or chalkboard

Caveats and Options

In this activity, students have an opportunity to listen to English in a real context, that of music. They are culturally immersed in the language for the length of one song. As they listen to the lyrics, they encounter patterns of speech and new expressions to add to their vocabulary base.

Procedure

1. Tune in a local radio station that features "oldies but goodies" from the 1960s and 1970s.
2. To initiate listening, ask the students to listen for familiar expressions between songs such as the name of the station, weather, date, time, and news briefs. Discuss briefly.
3. Have the students focus on listening to the songs played. Each student should write down everything she understands in English from the next song played, even if it is just one word or broken phrases.
4. The songs are usually short (2–3 minutes), so repeat this activity with several songs until the students are successful. Write along with them.
4. Turn the radio off or down and discuss what everyone wrote. Share the results on the board or overhead with the teacher and other students filling in gaps if possible.

1. The students may find this activity difficult at first, but with a little practice, they will soon sing along with the music. Many of these songs tell a story, which makes understanding easier and logical. Many songs also repeat phrases over and over. With some students you might find it helpful to record a segment of a radio broadcast so you can replay the same songs until the lyrics are complete.
2. Have the students work in groups to complete the lyrics to the song.

3. Assign a lyrics journal. You might give students five artists names (Elvis, the Beatles, the Mamas and Papas, the Animals, the Supremes) and require the lyrics to one song from each artist. This activity encourages further practice of listening skills and builds cultural knowledge.

4. If you find you need the lyrics to songs to answer questions from the students, a service on Internet gives you access to this information. At the % prompt of your access line, type this address:

telnet consultant.micro.umn.edu
Login as ''gopher''
Select ''Internet file server (ftp)sites/''
Select ''popular FTP Sites via gopher/''
Select ''lyrics/''
The rest is self-explanatory.

Contributor

Sharon Sealy, ABD, is currently researching academic competence in mainstream classrooms at the University of Georgia in the United States. Her interests include multicultural awareness and the Hispanic culture.

Going Home for Christmas

Levels
Advanced

Aims
Listen to native-speaker input
Learn cultural information
Practice top-down processing in listening comprehension
Develop skills in identifying similarities and differences and distinguishing between general and specific information

Class Time
55 minutes

Preparation Time
20–30 minutes

Resources
Audiotaped dialogue
Tape player
Task Sheets 1 and 2
(see Appendix)

In these activities, the learners gain interesting cultural information, and are exposed to different varieties of English.

Procedure

1. Tape a 14-minute dialogue about going home for Christmas in which two speakers, (e.g., an American and a Filipino) have a casual conversation about celebrating Christmas in their home countries.
2. Make a copy of Task Sheets 1 and 2 (see Appendix) for each learner.
3. Ask students to discuss the following with a partner (for about 10 minutes):

   Is Christmas celebrated in your home country? If so, how? What kinds of special food do you eat? What about clothing, food, places, people, customs . . .? If not, talk about any customary event celebrated in your home country that is comparable to Christmas, say, any significant social or religious event celebrated at home or place of work . . . . What are the clothing, food, places, people, and customs . . . in celebrating such an event?

4. Explain to the class some vocabulary associated with Christmas, such as *sumptuous, mass, stockings, godfathers, godmothers, Protestant, trimming, tone, undertaking, raked, shrieking, mad rush.*
5. With the class, look over Task Sheet 1. Have learners listen to the tape and check a list for similarities and differences. Repeat with Task Sheet 2, checking for specifics.
6. In groups, have learners compare their answers.

Caveats and Options

1. For low-level classes, play the tape once for very general listening and give out five true/false questions in a listening lesson immediately preceding this one.
2. Focus on nations other than the United States and the Philippines; alternatively, focus on other customary events. In either variation, speakers may follow the schema as set out in the task sheet below:

10-Minute Casual Conversation About Celebrating Christmas

Starter (2 minutes)

How to spend this Christmas: descriptions and attitudes.

Main Part (8 minutes)

How to celebrate Christmas back home (in the Philippines and the U.S.): descriptions, attitudes & comparison.

1. descriptions: clothing, food, places, people, customs . . . .
2. attitudes: agreement/disagreement; likes/dislikes.
3. comparison: similarities/differences; religious, sociocultural
   . . . .

During the taping, only the speakers have to be present in the production of semiauthentic, nonscripted input.

Appendix:
Task Sheets

The tape you'll be listening to soon is about Christmas. Two women, one from the Philippines and the other from the United States, talk about how they'll spend this Christmas. They'll also discuss how they normally celebrate Christmas back home in the Philippines and the United States. Comparisons are made in terms of food, gifts, clothing, social visits, and atmosphere at the place of work, etc. Listen to the tape while referring to the list below. There are descriptions (listed in the order of mention on the tape) that characterize how some Filipinos and/or some Americans spend their Christmas. Check the appropriate box to show which descriptions are part of the Filipino (F) and/or American (A) culture.

(continued)

Task Sheet 1

F	A	
		going home on the 19th
		enjoyable for kids
		"noche buena"
		big dinner
		stockings for gifts
		kids put on best dresses and clothes
		kids visit godfathers and godmothers
		kids collect money
		kids compete who got most gifts
		roast pork / beef stew / native cakes
		Christmas delicacy made from taro
		egg custard
		celebrating in more Protestant way
		couldn't open up gifts until everybody was up
		illegal to go and wake somebody up on Christmas morning
		allowing to have one person open a gift at a time
		family reunions and visiting friends
		celebration as a clan undertaking
		celebration from nuclear family to extended family
		going back home to provinces
		students fly home to the islands
		Dec. 24 almost always declared a half-working day
		Dec. 24 is usually a mad rush
		brandied egg nog / fruit cake / butter cookies in office
		big breakfast
		roast beef / pudding

Task Sheet 2

Listen to the tape and refer to the list on Task Sheet 1 for the second time. Some of the listed descriptions you've checked are shared by most Filipinos and/or most Americans in general; whereas others apply specifically to the speaker's own personal or family situation. Add a question mark to the already checked box to show that the description is true only for the speaker's specific situation.

Contributor

Wai-king Tsang is a Lecturer in the English Department, City University of Hong Kong. She holds an MA in ESOL from the University of Hawaii at Manoa in the United States.

Appreciating Advertisements

Levels
Intermediate

Aims
Become aware of the
way in which
advertisements work
Develop extensive and
intensive listening skills

Class Time
30 minutes

Preparation Time
15 minutes

Resources
Videotaped
advertisements from the
TV for the same product
type (e.g., cars, credit
cards, or washing
powder)

This activity raises the students' awareness of how language is manipulated for effect and helps them develop the ability to use the context to help decipher what they have heard.

Procedure

1. Discuss the main aims of advertising.
2. Ask questions such as "Does the style of advertising change depending on the product? Why do you think this is? Have you got any favorite advertisements? If so what are they and why do you like them? What do advertisers use to help you to remember their product?"
3. Explain that you are going to watch some advertisements for the same kind of product.
4. Play the tape and ask students to fill in the worksheet below:

Listening: Appreciating Advertisements

You are going to look at two or three ads advertising the same kind of product.

Watch the ads and fill in the chart below.

You will see the ads at least three times.

(continued)

Name	Sound Effects	Key Words/Script	Visual effects
1			
2			
3			

What is the key phrase/word for each ad?
What is the main emphasis of each ad?
Which do you prefer? Why?

5. Play the tape three times and pause it when necessary.
6. Ask students to discuss their answers in pairs and then as a class.

Caveats and Options

1. Choose some advertisements that are designed to appeal to men and some designed to appeal to women.
2. Ask students to note any differences in the language used.

Contributor

Jackie Wheeler lectures at Sir Robert Black College of Education, Hong Kong.

Part IV: Using Technology

Phone Mail

Levels
Intermediate

Aims
Learn to follow
instructions

Class Time
20-30 minutes

Preparation Time
30 minutes

Resources
Audiotape recorder
Deck of playing cards,
Numbers 1 (ace)–10

This task helps students learn how to deal with phone mail technology, which is rapidly expanding and can be intimidating.

Procedure

1. Select one local entity that uses phone mail (e.g., a bank) and develop several everyday situations for the students to respond to (e.g., calling a bank: "You want to know your account balance," "You wish to speak to someone in customer service"). Each situation should require a different response (i.e., a different button to push).
2. Call the entity and record several sequences that respond to the situations (preferably a speaker phone, if available). Several phone calls will be necessary to record submenus. If desired, prepare a simple chart or diagram to clarify the menu and submenus.
3. In class, give a brief explanation of how phone mail works. Introduce the business to be called in order to give students a chance to brainstorm vocabulary and functions (e.g., "Why would you call a bank?" "To ask about interest rates"; "To ask about my balance").
4. Place students in small groups. Hand out one set of cards per group.
5. Read a situation, play the tape through to the end of the first menu, and then pause the tape. Students must indicate their choice ("Which button would you press?") by holding up a card with the number.
6. After deciding which response is correct, start the tape and play the first submenu. Students make their choices as before.
7. After each situation, discuss correct and incorrect strategies in dealing with voice mail ("You should have pressed 1 for Account Balances instead of 2 for Commercial Transactions").

Contributor

Dennis Bricault teaches in North Park College, Chicago, in the United States.

Where's That Picture?

Levels
Any

Aims
Locate a picture by
listening to a
description
Learn to tolerate other
accents

Class Time
45 minutes–1 hour

Preparation Time
10 minutes

Resources
One picture for each
student
Language laboratory or
one numbered cassette
player with cassette and
earphones for each
learner

In the "Three Ps" of teaching (presentation, practice, and production), this activity falls into the production phase.

Procedure

1. Ask learners to choose a picture and to write a description of it. The length of the writing depends on the ability of the learner. The descriptions need only take in the form of the notes.
2. Have learners record their descriptions at their numbered consoles.
3. Collect the pictures and stick them to the board so that everyone can see them. Attach a letter to each one (e.g., A, B, C . . .)
4. Have learners move about the language lab listening to each other's descriptions and noting which picture is being described each time (e.g., Console 14 = Picture F).

Caveats and Options

1. Make this activity more difficult by using pictures that are more and more similar, as it is a more complex task to discern differences between, say, 15 pictures of kangaroos than to do so for 15 totally different pictures.
2. Make this activity into a creative listening task by asking learners to record a story about the picture they have. Successive listeners then have to locate the picture and continue the story on the cassette for the next listener.

Contributor

Ivano Buoro is Director of Studies at the Intensive English College in Sydney, Australia. He has taught EFL in Japan and Australia for more than 10 years.

At the Sound of the Beep . . .

Levels
Intermediate

Aims
Practice listening to and
getting information from
messages left on a
telephone answering
machine
Practice giving personal
information and talking
about future plans
Practice requests,
idioms, and reported
speech

Class Time
30 minutes–1 hour

Preparation Time
10 minutes

Resources
Answering machine

Procedure

1. Record some messages from an answering machine onto a tape.
2. Prepare a list of questions for students to discuss for each message (these can be put on a handout, written on the board, or presented orally). The type of questions you prepare will obviously depend on the language used in the messages and the level of your students (e.g., idioms for higher level classes).
3. In class discuss briefly the role of answering machines in Western society, including both their advantages and disadvantages.
4. Present the questions for the first message and then play it for the students as many times as they need to get down the necessary information.
5. Have students compare their answers in pairs or small groups and then go over them with the whole class. Clarify any new vocabulary.
6. Do the same with the rest of the messages.

Caveats and Options

1. Prepare an information table or a cloze, multiple choice, or true-false exercise for the students to fill out while they listen (depending on the level of the class).
2. For practice in reported speech, have the students give the messages to each other. You may need to practice some of the reductions involved, such as *Wha'd, What did* (e.g., "Bill called." "Oh, wha'd he say?" "He said that . . .").
3. After you have gone through all the messages, have pairs of students pick one of them and act out a short follow-up phone conversation.

You may need to go over some of the conventions used (e.g., ''Hi Jane, I got your message. What's up?'').

4. In order to have more control over the content of the messages, phone the answering machine yourself and leave a more scripted message that uses the language you want to deal with in class.

Contributor

Mark Dickens teaches at Fields College International, Victoria, Canada.

How's Your Love Life?

Levels
Intermediate +

Aims
Practice getting
information about
people from recorded
personal ads
Practice the language of
personal information,
personality
characteristics, hobbies
and interests, idioms,
and relative clauses

Class Time
1 hour

Preparation Time
Varies

Resources
Recorded personal ads
and some from
newspapers
Handouts

Procedure

1. Call up the phone personals in your local newspaper and listen to some of the recorded personal ads. Record several that you think would be appropriate (contentwise and levelwise) for your class.
2. Photocopy the particular written ads you have recorded or (if you don't want to give too many clues) any page of personal ads from the local paper.
3. Prepare handouts for your students to record the information from the personals on. This could be simply a series of headings (e.g., Name, Personality, Interests, Other Info) or something more elaborate (e.g., cloze, true/false, multiple choice, matching) . You may want to focus on relative clauses (e.g., ''He's looking for a person who likes to dance and read books'') or select some specific idioms or slang used in the ads.
4. Introduce the topic of personal ads by asking questions such as: Why do people put personal ads in the paper? Is it popular in your country? What do you think of the idea? Would you put such an ad in the paper? Would you answer one? (You will obviously need to adjust the questions to the specific teaching situation).
5. Look at the photocopied personal ads and go over the abbreviations used (e.g., SWF = single white female).
6. Hand out the exercise you have prepared for the students. You may also give them copies of the written ads they will be listening to in order to help them in getting the information for each one.
7. Have students compare their answers in pairs or small groups and then go over them with the whole class. Clarify any new vocabulary.
8. Do the same with the rest of the ads.

9. Conclude with a discussion about the ads they have listened to (e.g., What kind of people do you think they are? Would you like to meet them?).

Caveats and Options

1. To make the task a little more difficult, have the students initially match the recorded ads with the written ones (rather than telling them which one they are listening to). The difficulty of this activity will depend on the similarity between the two.
2. After you have gone through all the ads, pairs of students can pick one of them and act out a short follow-up phone conversation. You may need to go over some of the conventions used (e.g., "Hi, I read your ad in the paper . . . ").
3. As a possible follow-up writing activity, have the students write a short imaginary biography of one of the people they listened to.
4. You will obviously need to be selective in choosing which ads to use, as some will be inappropriate, especially in certain cultural situations.

Contributor

Mark Dickens teaches at Fields College International, Victoria, Canada.

Telephone Info Lines

Levels
Intermediate +

Aims
Practice getting
information about
current events through
recorded messages
Practice the language of
dates, times, names,
places, and numbers

Class Time
30 minutes

Preparation Time
30 minutes

Resources
Local telephone
information line
Handouts

Procedure

1. Telephone the local telephone information line in your community (sometimes called the *Talking Yellow Pages*) and note down the basic menu choices (i.e., the buttons that must be pressed to get the different topics), the specific information you want your students to listen for, and any words or phrases you hear that may be problematic for the students.
2. Prepare any handout you will need for the exercise, keeping in mind that the information is probably updated every week or so. As an initial task, students could match the menu numbers with the topic headings in the main menu, fill in a table with information (e.g., given the names of theaters in town, fill in the movies playing, times, and ratings, or fill in the weather forecast for specific days and places, including conditions, highs and lows) or listen for answers to specific questions (e.g., When can you see *Phantom of the Opera* at the Playhouse?).
3. In the class introduce the topic of telephone information lines and find out if the students have used them in their native language. Talk about what kind of information you can find out through such information lines (e.g., weather, sports scores, entertainment information, soap opera updates).
4. Hand out the exercise to be completed for homework, and clarify that the students understand it. Go over any vocabulary involved (both on the sheet and what they may hear on the phone), prepare them for any problematic words or phrases they may hear, and ensure that the students understand how to use the information line (including how to get back to the main menu or repeat a selection).

5. Encourage the students to note down information in addition to what you have asked for and to come to class with any questions they have about what they heard on the phone.
6. Follow up in the next class by going over the answers to the exercise and discussing any questions raised by the students.

Caveats and Options

1. As a follow-up, pairs of students can pick one of the items they have listened to and act out a short phone conversation, perhaps calling someone to find out more information about it.
2. These information lines are available in most major cities in North America and are a relatively nonthreatening way for students to get information over the phone without talking to a live person. The beauty of them is that the students can listen to the information as many times as they need to complete the task. Because these information lines only work on touch-tone phones, make sure that all the students have access to one in order to do their homework.

Contributor

Mark Dickens teaches at Fields College International, Victoria, Canada.

Using Vibrotactile Aids

Levels
Intermediate

Aims
Perceive sentence
rhythm and intonation

Class Time
1–1 1/2 hours

Preparation Time
1 hour

Resources
Audiotaped alpha and
baroque music
Body Sonic Chair
Verbotonal Filter (slope
.52 db/Oct., LPF 300
HZ, HPF 3,000 HZ)
Sound imprint cards

This activity helps students learn to distinguish low-frequency sounds so that they can hear sentence rhythm and intonation.

Procedure

1. Prior to instruction, play alpha or baroque music to allow the chair to vibrate and the learners to relax. At this time, have the learners do neck, shoulder and waist stretches.
2. Repeat some simple to complex sentences several times with the SONY repeater. Do not allow learners to read the sentences.
3. Repeat some sentences using the vibrotactile aid and the low pass filter simultaneously.
4. Play the normal sentence sounds and the filter sentence sounds alternately. Students listen to the filter sounds, trying to repeat the sentences without looking at them.
5. In the final stage, ask the learners to repeat, listening only to the filter sentence sounds with the vibrotactile aid.

Caveats and Options

According to Guberina (1961), low-frequency vibrations can instruct people effectively in rhythm and intonation. Body Sonic in Japan has studied and developed a chair with a vibrator that can produce such vibrations. This chair can be useful for rhythmical training. Another effective instrument is the verbotonal filter, which abstracts only the low-frequency sound area of a given sound. Lozanov (1982) advocates the use of alpha and baroque music, which are employed in suggestopedia. These kinds of music seem to reduce the learners' anxiety and enable them to relax.

References and Further Reading

Guberina, P. (1961). La methode audio-visuelle structuro-globale et ses implications dans l'enseignementde la phonetique. *Studia Romanica et Anglica Zagrabiensia*, 10-43.

Lozanov, G. (1982). Suggestology and suggestopedy. In R. W. Blair (Ed.), *Innovative approaches to language teaching* (pp. 146-159). New York: Newbury House.

Roberge, C. (1979). *Hatsuon kyosei to gogaku kyoiku*. Tokyo: Taishukan.

Contributors

Yasuharu Kiji is a Lecturer at Baika Women's College, Ibaraki, Japan. Maidy Giber Kiji is a Lecturer at Konan Women's University, Kobe, Japan.

Listening to the News

Levels
Intermediate

Aims
Listen to high density input
Listen to daily news broadcasts

Class Time
45 minutes

Preparation Time
30 minutes

Resources
Video cassette recorder
Videotape of current news broadcast

This activity can provide students with a very reinforcing real-life achievement. Although a number of books teach news listening, this procedure is flexible enough to be adapted to any news broadcast, even current news.

Procedure

1. Explain the listening task to the students. Have the students list basic categories of news features on the chalkboard. Be sure that these include disasters, crimes, wars, VIPs, and human interest stories.
2. Play a news segment that includes video of the story being described. Ask the students what basic category the story belongs to.
3. Suggest that the students listen again. This time have them listen for when and where the story happened and who was involved.
4. Ask the students to suggest what the next development in the story will be.
5. Proceed to a second news segment. After covering a number of types of news stories, make the task more difficult by selecting a story that is only read by the anchor without video from the scene.
6. Suggest that the students follow up on one of the stories by listening to the news as homework.

Caveats and Options

Use an audiotape of a radio news broadcast.

Contributor

Hugh Rutledge graduated from Boston University in 1988. He has taught in East Asia for several years and is Head of Faculty at Tokyo International College, in Japan.

211

Using Films in Advanced Listening Courses

Levels
Advanced

Aims
Develop the ability to understand and enjoy films
Improve comprehension of natural conversational English

Class Time
8 hours/film

Preparation Time
4-5 hours/new film

Resources
Library of films or television programs on videotape
Videotape player (VCR) with audio output jack
Audiotape recorder with audio input jack
Capacity to copy audiotapes
Capacity to produce and copy printed material

Films can provide a vivid introduction to Western culture, and they are always more interesting than most materials for teaching English—after all, they are designed to entertain. As language-teaching material, they provide a good transition between the slow, clear "teacher talk" of the classroom and the natural English of typical native conversation.

An advantage of this approach is that it helps students guess throughout the film, rather than clumping assistance toward the beginning. Second, and perhaps even more important, the method preserves the integrity of a film by allowing it to be shown as a whole. This, in turn, helps the film retain its appeal and the students a high level of motivation.

Procedure

I. Preparation

1. Select a film with the (a) difficulty of the language (speed, accent, sound clarity, vocabulary), (b) cultural difficulty of the film (background knowledge), and (c) appeal of the film in mind. Before choosing a film, view it with teaching specifically in mind; half-remembered impressions of films are often unreliable. (For example, I thought *E.T.* would be an ideal film until I watched it carefully and realized that most of the dialogue consisted of short rapid bursts of very colloquial U.S. teenagers' English.)

2. Watch the film while taking notes as to the location on the VCR counter, the length, and the content of the film dialogues. (Also note potential comprehension questions—see below.) Then record 8-12 scenes onto the cassette tape. The scenes should be evenly spaced throughout the film so as to present a rough outline of the plot without giving away all of the story and should include major turning points

of the plot, key vocabulary items, and important scenes that are particularly difficult to understand (e.g., shouted arguments). The total length of the tape should be around 8-12 minutes; if the tape becomes too long, the workload for students becomes excessive.

3. Record the scenes you want directly from the videotape onto an audiotape using patch cords and the audio output jack on the back of the VCR. Be sure to leave a few seconds of blank tape between each scene—if they all run together, the tape is much more confusing for students. (Although such use of a film sound track is probably within the bounds of fair use of copyrighted material, you might want to check to make sure that in your country recording these segments of the film sound track for educational use is legal.)

4. Prepared printed materials to accompany the cassette tape: (a) a list of main characters in the film; (b) a brief introduction to each scene on the cassette tape, identifying the speakers and explaining what is going on; (c) a list of key vocabulary words and glosses for each scene (in addition to printing this, it is also a good idea to record the words onto the tape so that students can hear as well as see them); and (d) comprehension questions. You might choose to have one or two comprehension questions after each scene on the cassette tape to help students focus their listening. More important, prepare a list of questions covering the whole film that students can try to answer either as they view it or afterward.

II. Implementation

1. Prepare the students by having them study the materials. Listening to the tape is generally hard work because dialogues that would have been difficult enough to follow if seen in the context of the film are now even more difficult once they are deprived of their visual clues. To some extent, this problem can be resolved by the written materials prepared to accompany the tape, and by the fact that students can listen to the taped scenes as many times as they need to. However, working with these tapes still generally requires serious effort, and this part of the task is decidedly more work than fun.

2. There are a variety of ways to cover a film in class, but a typical approach consists of four 2-hour class periods as follows:

   a. Go over the tape with students, answering questions and explaining whatever is still unclear.
   b. Show the film in its entirety. During or after the viewing, have students answer the comprehension questions. It is vital to obtain the best possible listening conditions. Poor sound quality resulting from a small speaker in a large room often drastically reduces students' chances of understanding dialogue. Sound quality can be improved by running the audio through a stereo or PA system, and if a film is shown in a listening laboratory, the audio can often be run through the system so that students can listen on headphones.
   c. Discuss the film.
   d. View the film a second time. It is generally advisable to show a film more than once because students will often pick up many things they missed the first time, a process that is both educational and encouraging.

III. Assessment

1. Follow up with brief quizzes consisting of comprehension questions, summary writing, or review writing. In order for this approach to film teaching to work, it is important that students invest serious time and effort in working with the taped and written materials before viewing the film. Brief quizzes, consisting of comprehension questions, can motivate students to invest time in preparation. Quizzes scheduled at the beginning of the first period, before you have gone over the tape with students, will encourage students to work hard at home; quizzes scheduled at the end of the first period will motivate students to ask questions in class. It is generally best if these quizzes cover the main points of the dialogue segments included on the tape rather than minor details; the former type of quiz is sufficient to encourage students to invest time working with the prepared materials, whereas the latter tends to force students into excessive attention to detail.

2. In order to encourage students to work with the tapes and written materials, it may be wise on a final or midterm examination to include some vocabulary and comprehension questions covered by the tapes and written material. However, the ultimate goal of this teaching approach is to build students' ability to understand a film as a whole, a process of which guessing is a major part, and the best comprehensive test for film listening skills is to simply show a film which students have not yet seen (either with or without having first studied tapes and materials you prepare) and then test for comprehension. Testing could consist of either answers to comprehension questions, or written summaries of the film (the latter exercise would encourage students to take notes).

3. A good alternative to the testing approach suggested above is to combine your film course with writing by having students write film reviews. This not only gives you a good idea of how well students understood the film but also helps students develop critical analysis and expository writing skills.

Contributor

Don Snow works for the Overseas Liaison Office of the Amity Foundation as Coordinator for the Teachers Project, a program through which language teachers work in China.

News Items

Levels
Intermediate

Aims
Develop extensive and
intensive listening skills

Class Time
25 minutes

Preparation Time
15–20 minutes

Resources
Recorded news items
from the radio and TV
Prepared worksheet
showing brief headlines
from the news in
jumbled order
Several true/false
statements about the
news items

This activity helps develop students' awareness of the various ways in which people listen. Sometimes they need to listen for the general meaning, whereas on other occasions they are more concerned with specific information.

Procedure

1. Distribute the headline worksheet to the students. Ask them to look at the headlines and make predictions about what they will hear in the news item (this can be done in pairs, groups, or as a whole-class activity).
2. Tell the students to number the news items (1, 2, 3 . . .) as they hear them on the news report. Play the tape and then check the answers with the class.
3. Distribute the true/false worksheet and ask the students to read over the statements.
4. Play the tape a second time and ask the students to write T or F next to the statements. Check the answers around the class. It is useful to write some ambiguous statements that can be either true or false so that there is some discussion about the correct answer. Listen to the tape again to, check the answers.
5. Tell the students to listen to the tape one more time. This time they should try to make their own notes.
6. Arrange the students into groups to discuss their notes and perhaps produce their own version of the news.

Contributors

Jackie Wheeler lectures at Sir Robert Black College of Education, Hong Kong. Austin Conway is Language Instructor at the Hong Kong University of Science and Technology.

Using Videos

Levels
Any

Aims
Identify key concepts
Make inferences
Listen for details

Class Time
35–40 minutes

Preparation Time
15-20 minutes

Resources
Suitable video

The use of video in listening activities adds visual appeal and helps students understand the spoken material better. This method of "listening" to the video before the actual viewing aims at arousing the students' interest and motivating them to listen in a meaningful context.

Procedure

1. In preparation, review the video and prepare a few general questions to help the students focus their attention. For example, where are the characters? What are they doing? Who are these people? Also prepare a short worksheet based on the story in the video—comprehension questions in the form of multiple choices or short questions. Write down the vocabulary items and language items extracted from the video.
2. Explain to the students that before seeing the picture, they will be listening to the sound of the video only. Put the prepared general questions (and the title of the video, if there is one) on the board to help the students figure out more easily what the video is about.
3. Cover the screen of the television and play the video.
4. After the first listening, check the students' comprehension and see if they can answer the questions on the board. The students are free to use their imagination and clues (from what they have heard in the video) to make guesses and infer what is happening.
5. Play the video again, with the picture, and let the students compare what they imagined and what they actually see in the sequence.
6. Discuss the sequence with the students. Introduce specific vocabulary items, language items/functions, special rhetorical devices, and expressions used in that particular situation.

7. Give out the worksheet and tell the students to complete it. (If necessary, play the video again.)
8. Check and discuss the answers with the students.

Caveats and Options

1. Choose videos that are short (approximately 5 minutes), situational (e.g., in the supermarket, in the office, in the salon), and in the mode of a short story or episode.
2. The worksheet must include the following:

   a. specific actions in the video that the students rearrange according to sequence
   b. excerpts of conversations that the students to rearrange according to order
   c. comprehension questions in the form of multiple choice or short answer questions.

References and Further Reading

The British Council. (1994). *Video English*. London: The British Council/Macmillan.

Contributor

Matilda M. W. Wong is Assistant Lecturer in the Department of English, City University of Hong Kong.

Part V: Listening for Academic Purposes

Building Formal Information Schema

Levels
Advanced

Aims
Develop awareness of segmentation and hierarchy of information in lectures
Listen for more than the main ideas of an academic lecture

Class Time
Varies

Preparation Time
Varies

Resources
Videotaped academic lecture segments
Transcripts of certain portions of the segments
Overhead projector

Procedure

1. Define the following information moves, giving markers, both explicit (introductory words, phrases, or sentences) and implicit (e.g., louder word emphasis, longer word emphasis, longer pause, repetition, place in hierarchy). Use the style(s) of presentation of information used in the videotaped portion(s) of the module.

   Topic Announcement
   Expansion
   Restatement or Paraphrase
   Example
   Summary
   Topic Shift

   Other less important moves to mention are digression, return to topic, and postponement.

2. Record a short section of a lecture.
3. Select which discourse types to teach: definition sequences, classification sequences, explanation sequences, process sequences, and so forth.
4. Transcribe the section or sections to use in class. These transcripts do not have to be exacting, but should include nearly every word.
5. Go over the first few transcript segments with the class using an overhead projector. These can be done as (a) multiple choice on each individual move, (b) a list for whether a move is present or not, (c) multiple choice on which move sequence is the correct sequence, or (d) a chart to identify the move and what the important information is in that move. (See Appendix.)

6. With short transcripts of lecture segments, practice move identification/sequencing in small groups and discuss the results in a large group.
7. Use videotaped segments for the above exercise types instead of transcripts for 1- to 3-minute sequences.
8. Play a new videotape and have the students take notes from it. Then have the students reconstruct the information in key word outline form.

Caveats and Options

1. Have students predict what move or what information could come next.
2. Substitute questioning as to how a topic announcement is introduced, how many examples are given, whether the information is repeated, and so forth for move identification in videotaped segments.
3. Using the outlines to make formal written summaries is a good way to illustrate the differences between spoken and written information.
4. Other exercise types (fill in blanks, rearranging information, identification of order of information) can also be successfully used.
5. Content of lectures should be general (e.g., not mechanics of solids)—unless all the students are engineers.

Appendix: Sample Text and Exercise Types

A. Identifying the Move Function in Isolation

1. OK. Now they throw some more terms at us, What does *synchronous* mean?

   a. Topic announcement
   b. Digression
   c. Expansion

2. This was Memorial Day weekend. The only thing you could find on television were old John Wayne war movies. They were celebrating Memorial Day, you see.

   a. Expansion
   b. Digression
   c. Example

3. There's always one great scene when they say "synchronize your watches." What are they doing? When they're synchronizing their watches they're aligning them up to a specific time and that's what we do when we synchronize computers. Yes?

   a. Summary
   b. Topic Shift
   c. Expansion

4. Student: Is it done in the same way?
   Professor: Uh, well, uh, Let's talk about that later.

   a. Topic Shift
   b. Digression
   c. Postponement

5. Anyway, where were we? Oh yeah.

   a. Expansion
   b. Return to Topic
   c. Summary

6. When we are sending from computer (a) to computer (b) or from a computer to a printer, if we're synchronized, it means its timed.

   a. Expansion
   b. Example
   c. Summary

7. Ok, any questions? Let's go on.

   a. Return to Topic
   b. Topic Shift
   c. Topic Announcement

B. Presence of Move

   Topic Announcement
   Expansion
   Restatement
   Example

Postponement
Digression
Return to Topic
Summary
Topic Shift

C. Multiple Choice of Hierarchy of Moves

1. Topic	2. Topic
Announcement	Announcement
Expansion	Digression
Expansion	Expansion
Postponement	Postponement
Expansion	Return to Topic
Topic Shift	Summary
Topic	Topic Shift
Announcement	

D. Move Identification With Information

Move Type	Information in Move
1.	
2.	
3.	
4.	
5.	
6.	
7.	

Contributor

James E. Bame is Senior Lecturer in the Intensive English Language Institute of Utah State University in the United States.

Pause and Paraphrase

Levels
High intermediate +

Aims
Improve lecture note-taking speed and accuracy

Class Time
45 minutes

Preparation Time
15–30 minutes

Resources
A short (5- to 15-minute) academic lecture appropriate to students' interests
Tape recorders or language laboratory facilities

Language students may have reasonable comprehension of academic lectures but often find they don't have enough time to simultaneously form a mental paraphrase of the information and make an accurate note of it. Providing opportunities to practice these skills should eventually produce better note-takers.

Procedure

1. Engage the students with warm-up and/or prelistening tasks of your choice.
2. Arrange students into groups of four or five.
3. Provide each group with the same recorded lecture.
4. Have students listen to each segment, then pause at an appropriate place in the talk. At each pause, have students take turns verbally paraphrasing the segment they have just listened to. As a student paraphrases a lecture segment, the other students take notes. Each group moves at its own pace, but encouraged students (over several lessons using different lectures) to paraphrase more quickly without sacrificing accuracy. If desired, have one student in the group time the paraphrasers. Over subsequent lessons, students should see their time improve. You can discourage rewinding by reminding students that they cannot rewind a real lecture.
5. After they've finished listening to the tape, ask each group, working from their individual notes, to produce a complete version. A group scribe could do this on an overhead projector transparency or on a flip chart.
6. Have the class compare their notes by identifying any gaps or inconsistencies between groups.

Caveats and Options

1. Initially students may need some guidance in the form of an outline with missing information that they have to fill in. (See the Appendix for a sample handout.) As students improve in their note-taking skills, you can pare down these information-gap handouts and eventually eliminate them.

2. A variation of the above technique identifies discourse markers in lectures (e.g., *Another point . . ., Okay, the next thing . . .*). With this task, students, not the teacher, decide when to pause based on the lecturer's use of discourse markers. And instead of paraphrasing, students only note the key point(s) in each segment to produce an outline. Longer lectures (20 minutes) work best for this type of lesson (see Lebauer, 1988).

3. Good sources of recorded lectures are Adkins and Mckean (1983), Lebauer (1988), Lynch (1983), and Roguski and Palmberg (1990). Another source is radio or TV broadcasts of university lectures.

References and Further Reading

Adkins, A., & McKean, I. (1983). *Text to note*. London: Edward Arnold.

Lebauer, S. R. (1988). *Learn to listen; listen to learn*. Englewood Cliffs, NJ: Prentice Hall.

Lynch, T. (1983). *Study listening*. Cambridge: Cambridge University Press.

Roguski, C., & Palmberg, E. (1990). *Academic mini-lectures*. New York: Maxwell Macmillan.

Appendix: Sample Information-Gap Handout

Renewal Processes

Defining a Renewal Process:

Two Types:

    1.
    2.

    Renewal Function:

    Elementary Renewal Theorem:

The Economy of Renewal Processes
    Reward: The Ideal Taxi Driver's Income
    Expectations and Conditional Expectations
    Renewal Reward Theorem: Hourly Income

    Concluding remarks:
    Adapted from unpublished lecture notes written by Liming Liu, Department of Industrial Engineering, Hong Kong University of Science and Technology

Contributor

Maureen Brown is Assistant Instructor in the Language Centre at Hong Kong University of Science and Technology. She has taught in China, Canada, and most recently, Hong Kong. She thanks Sarah Carmichael and Liming Liu for their help.

Famous People

Levels
Low intermediate

Aims
Develop skill in taking
notes from a short talk

Class Time
10–15 minutes

Preparation Time
15–30 minutes

Resources
Audiotape of a short
account of a famous
person's life
Copies of a
chronological table

This exercise gives students who need to learn English for academic purposes the opportunity to develop their skills in listening for the main points of information and in recording these points succinctly.

Procedure

1. Elicit from the students what they already know about the personality you are going to present.
2. Give out copies of the table below and explain the procedure.

Year	Event	Place
1862		
	wrote first novel	
		Paris

3. Play the tape while students fill in Column 1.
4. Play the tape again as students complete Column 2.
5. Play the tape a third time while students finish Column 3 and check their work.

Caveats and Options

Have the students work in groups and think up their own famous person. They should talk about this person and make notes on a table similar to that above. One student from the group then stands up and talks about the person while the rest of the class listen and complete a chronological table for the people described. A class discussion can then take place about the accuracy of the information in the tables.

Contributor

Dominic Cogan is a Lecturer in English at Fukui Prefecural University, Japan. Previously, he has worked in TESOL in Ireland, Ghana, and Oman.

In a Nutshell

Levels
High intermediate +

Aims
Practice listening and
summarizing

Class Time
25–30 minutes

Preparation Time
Varies

Resources
Audiotaped
conversation

Students need practice listening selectively to extended discourse. Native speakers can filter out what they don't need to hear, but nonnative speakers often get bogged down (and very tired) trying to listen for and understand every word. In this exercise, students listen for key points and ignore unnecessary detail and redundancy.

Procedure

1. Choose an audiotaped conversation (or write and record one) that contains both key and unnecessary information. An ideal conversation would involve two speakers with identifiably different voices (e.g., one female and one male) discussing the same topic from contrasting perspectives. For example, if the speakers are talking about their vacations, one could describe a package tour and the other a camping trip.
2. Tell your students that after they hear the conversation, they will summarize the key points the speakers made. While listening, students should focus on the main points only. If necessary, give your students some help by writing some subheadings on the board, for example (continuing the vacation theme):

    location
    weather
    accommodation
    food
    daily activities
    shopping
    expenses
    night life

3. Play the tape through once or twice. Have students note under each subheading one or two essential points each speaker made.
4. Working in pairs and using their notes, students summarize what the speakers said. Students then compare which points they considered most important and give reasons for their choices.

Contributor

Jonathan Hull is a doctoral candidate at the University of Bristol, UK. He has taught ESOL in Europe, the Middle East, East Asia, and the Pacific. He is one of the coauthors (under Jack C. Richards) of Interchange *(Cambridge University Press).*

Video Comprehension

Levels
Advanced

Aims
Understand and use the language of a technical demonstration

Class Time
1 hour

Preparation Time
30 minutes, excluding video production time

Resources
A 4- to 5-minute videotape of a technical demonstration
Photocopied task sheets for each member of the class (see Appendix)

Tertiary-level students frequently have problems understanding and following a technical demonstration. They need practice in guessing about new vocabulary and in understanding the discourse feature of a demonstration.

Procedure

1. Explain to the students what they will be viewing and why.
2. Hand out the task sheets (see Appendices A and B) and explain to the students what they will be expected to do.
3. The first task on the task sheet should be a list of key topic words used in the video demonstration (Appendix B). Ask the students to look at the words, but do not explain any of them at this stage. Tell the students that you will play the videotape once. As they listen, they should tick the words they hear on their task sheet.
4. Pair the students up and ask them to look at the vocabulary. Tell them to discuss the meaning of the words. If they are not sure, they should think about what they saw and consider any clues in the video that might help them guess the meaning of the words.
5. Bring the class together to discuss the vocabulary. Encourage the students to describe what they saw and heard on the video that will help them understand the words.
6. Focus the students' attention on the guided note-taking task on the task sheet (see Appendix B). Tell them that you will play the video recording again and that they should try to complete the skeleton notes.
7. Play the video the second time pausing to allow them time to complete their notes. Then play the video again without pausing, so that they can check their notes.
8. Ask the students to check their notes with a partner.

9. Tell the students to use their notes and work in pairs to try to give a talk similar to the one on the video. One student should give the talk while the other listens and checks from his notes.

10. Ask for a volunteer. Tell her that you are going to play the video again, but this time without any sound. The volunteer should try to add the commentary while the video is playing. The rest of the class can watch the video and listen to the new sound track. Do this several times with different volunteers.

Appendix A: Sample Vocabulary Items From a Video on Design

Key words overview

Tick these words and phrases as you hear them:

horizontal axis
contrast in the design
smaller typeface
minor secondary axis
reading heading
primary heading
spatial planes
contrasts in the design

Appendix B: Sample Guided Note-Taking Exercise

Guided note-taking

1. Introduction
   We're going to . . .
   You can see also . . . because the designer has used . . .

2. The Design
   The designer has a long
   We could say that, well,
   But the primary is
   The information is also

Contributor

Rena Kelly is Senior Lecturer in the Language and Communication Division and Coordinator of the Centre for Individual Language Learning at Temasek Polytechnic, Singapore.

Improving Aural Comprehension of Higher Numbers

Levels
Intermediate +

Aims
Develop skill in understanding numbers in the thousands, millions, billions, and higher when spoken at normal conversational speed

Class Time
5–10 minutes/class until mastery

Preparation Time
None

Resources
None

Most ESOL students handle numbers well in written form although there are some differences in usage of periods and commas in certain parts of the world. Becoming proficient in understanding the higher numbers takes practice.

Procedure

1. Select a number at random, beginning in the hundreds.
2. Provide students with scrap paper to write their numbers on.
3. Dictate the number to the students at normal conversational speed. This is crucial.
4. Continue dictating the number repeatedly as you walk around the room evaluating what the students are writing.
5. After several repetitions of the number, inspect each student's number (keep up the number repetition while doing this). If you detect an error, indicate the place of the error with the point of a pencil and with a shake of the head inform the student of the error. Move on to the next student and repeat the process if necessary.
6. After most students have finally understood the number, call on a student who has the number incorrectly written down to come to the chalkboard and write down her number. Ask the class for agreement or disagreement.
7. Ask a student with the correct number to come to the chalkboard and write his number next to the incorrect one. Go to the chalkboard and say both numbers several times to give practice in hearing the contrasts between the two numbers.
8. Continue the practice daily gradually moving into higher and higher numbers until the students are able to handle any numbers dictated with precision.

Caveats and Options

1. Never repeat parts of numbers—say the entire number at normal conversational speed so that students eventually learn how to handle the morphophonemic changes that occur in spoken numbers just as they do in other aspects of speech. By doing this, the students will be prepared to understand entire numbers rather than parts of them.
2. Dictate numbers embedded in a context. This variation requires additional preparation time.

Contributor

Ted Plaister is the retired founding chair of the Department of ESOL, University of Hawaii, in the United States. He is the author of ESOL Case Studies: The Real World of L2 Teaching and Administration *(Regents Prentice Hall).*

Experiencing America

ESOL students in mainstream classes must often understand and take notes from a lecture. By listening to this audiotape, the students can be exposed to a different voice and speed of speech to obtain important information about the state in which they reside. In this way, they learn history as they improve their listening skills.

Procedure

1. Ask students to follow along a map of their state as the narrator of the tape describes the towns and cities on an audio tour. They should actually trace with a pencil the trail described on the tape as the narrator moves from one town to the next. Have students share and discuss their maps.
2. Ask students to record the facts described on the tape about each city and town, sharing and verifying facts after each listening session.

Caveats and Options

Keep sessions short until the students are successful at mapping the trail. If students are truly lost, play the tape over again. When they are comfortable recognizing the names of towns and cities and following directions, such as *go north* or *just south of Atlanta*, then ask them to take further notes. The sessions should get longer until the students are comfortable with at least a 15-minute lecture, depending on the age group.

Experience America, Inc. has created an audiotape for each state plus the District of Columbia. The tapes are interesting and relate historical facts

**References
and Further
Reading**

and trivia about each state. To order a tape for your class, contact your library or write to the company:

Experience America, Inc.
P.O. Box 250
Cedar City, UT 84721

Contributor

Sharon Sealy, ABD, is currently researching academic competence in mainstream classrooms at the University of Georgia in the United States. Her interests include multicultural awareness and Hispanic culture.

Listening Cloze Dictation

Levels
Low intermediate +

Aims
Practice acquiring and using microskills relevant to academic listening
Develop basic note-taking strategies

Class Time
Lecture: 20–30 minutes
Follow-up activities: 30 minutes

Preparation Time
45 minutes-1 hour

Resources
Text from a magazine or book at a suitable reading level

For instruction in listening comprehension to be effective, teachers, especially lecturers, must anticipate their L2 students' receptive capabilities and provide adequately simplified input for the students to recall or retain the information presented.

Procedure

1. Select a section of text that includes a suitable topic or presentation or prepare an original draft.
2. Prepare a typed outline for the lecture presentation.
3. Construct a cloze version of the outline.
4. Provide a short vocabulary list (with definitions) of difficult words at the bottom of the outline.
5. Prepare a student worksheet (approximately 10 questions) based on the outline/lecture.
6. Prepare a "team" worksheet (a larger size) copy of the student worksheet with four spaces for the names of each group member.
7. Explain to the students that they will hear a short lecture about a certain topic in the form of a dictation and that, as students listen to the lecture, they are to write the words they hear in the blank spaces of the outline.
8. Go over the vocabulary list with the class.
9. Present the dictation three times. Use elaboration during the second presentation to incorporate discourse markers, pauses, redundancy, rhetorical questions, and appropriate nonverbal cues into the lecture.
10. Divide the class into groups of four students. Allow students to compare their outlines with others in the group. Circulate among the groups to answer questions and provide additional information.

11. Distribute the worksheet. Instruct students to complete the worksheet individually by referring to their outlines (or assign it as homework).
12. Check to see that all students have completed their individual worksheets. Distribute the team worksheet. Instruct students to use their individual worksheets to compare answers, formulate the best response to each question and select one group member to be a recorder.
13. Collect the team worksheets. Identify errors and write cues for correction.
14. Return worksheets for self-correction and peer feedback by group members.
15. Have the groups return corrected team worksheets to you for additional correction, if any.
16. Have students use the final, corrected version to correct individual worksheets.

Caveats and Options

1. Go over team worksheets orally, asking a group to respond to a question.
2. Have groups ask questions of members within their group or of other groups.
3. More advanced materials may be adapted and simplified.

Contributor

Stephen Timson is a member of the Faculty of Political Science and Business at Meiji University, Tokyo, Japan.

What's My Teacher Like?

Levels
Low intermediate

Aims
Develop note-taking
skills, careful listening,
and question-asking
strategies to fill in gaps
in lecture notes

Class Time
13–25 minutes

Preparation Time
5 minutes

Resources
Lecture about the
teacher written by the
teacher

**Caveats and
Options
Contributor**

Most students are very interested in learning more about their teacher. Using the teacher's life and information as material to be presented in a lecture can help motivate them to take notes and ask questions. This activity is a good starting point for students to practice taking notes on academic topics.

Procedure

1. Prepare and give a short lecture about yourself, leaving out some pertinent information. Instruct students to take notes as they listen.
2. After the lecture, divide the students into groups to write questions that you did not answer and that they would like you to answer on the particular topic(s) covered by your lecture only.
3. Allow the groups to ask their questions.
4. Tell the students that you will answer questions only on topics that you did not already address in your lecture.
5. Request input from the other students each time a question is asked. Say "Did I answer that question?" "Is it about the topic?" Answer the questions that the group deems answerable according to the rules you have set out.
6. Ask the group how they decided when a question was answerable. Discuss the importance of asking for clarification and determining a question's pertinence in any academic setting.

Once students are comfortable with taking notes and asking questions, use an academic topic.

Cindy Mckeag Tsukamoto is Assistant Professor of ESOL at Roosevelt University, Chicago, in the United States. She is the coauthor, with Sally La Luzerne-Oi, of Tell Me About It *(Heinle & Heinle).*

Part VI: Listening for Fun

Could You Repeat That, Please?

Levels
Beginning

Aims
Practice asking someone
to repeat something
Overcome anxiety about
not having understood
an utterance
Practice speaking up
more confidently

Class Time
20 minutes

Preparation Time
10 minutes

Resources
None

One of the main benefits of this activity is that students can use the questions immediately in any situation. This activity shows them that the reason they have not understood an utterance is not always because they do not know the language but because they simply did not hear (or listen to) what was said. By asking for a repetition, they can easily solve the problem.

Procedure

1. Write on the board a list of the responses that students need to be able to use when they haven't understood an utterance and want it repeated. Possible responses (for this level) include:

   Excuse me.
   What did you say?
   Excuse me. What did you say?
   Sorry, I couldn't hear you.
   Sorry?
   Could you repeat that, please?
   I beg your pardon.

2. Divide the class into two teams. Have the teams line up as far as possible from each other on opposite sides of the room. The configuration will look something like this:

A	1
B	2
C	3
D	4

3. Have students work in pairs with one student standing across the room from the other. Thus, Student A will work with Student 1, B with 2, and so on.

Student A begins by asking a question or giving a command in a low (but reasonably audible) voice. Student 1 must answer the question or complete the command. If Student 1 is not able to do this, she can take one step forward toward Student A and then has to ask Student A to repeat what he said. The goal is to understand as quickly as possible.

Caveats and Options

1. Have Student 2 help Student 1 by telling her what Student A said: "She said 'open the door'."
2. Have all of the students talk at the same time. This results in a great deal of background noise (which more closely resembles the real world), and students cannot hear as well and have to ask the speaker to repeat.

Contributor

Nadine Battaglia is a French and English Instructor at Language Academy, in Maebeshi, Japan. She previously taught French as a second language in France.

Listening to Songs

Levels
High intermediate

Aims
Develop intensive
listening skills by
listening to a song

Class Time
30 minutes

Preparation Time
10–20 minutes

Resources
Recording of a popular
song
Cassette player

Listening to songs in English is a popular classroom activity with many students. Although the song may be long, many of the lines are repeated, so the task is not as daunting as it first appears.

Procedure

1. Type a tapescript of the song you want to use. Double space so that students can write on the page. Change some of the words in the tapescript. Try to use words to make the changes sound like the original (e.g., *whispers* could be changed to *whiskers*, *gonna get you* to *gonna get two*). Make enough copies for the class.
2. Begin by talking about popular songs. Find out what the students know about the song they are about to hear.
3. Write the title on the board and get students to predict some of the words they might hear. Write up as many words as the students give you. Leave all the words on the board and play the song. Lead into group or class discussion about the words on the board that they *did not* hear in the song. Play the song again to check that certain words are not in the song.
4. Hand out the tapescript. Tell the students that some of the words have been changed. Inform the class that the task is to listen to the song again and change the incorrect words on the tapescript.
5. Have students check their corrections with a partner or in groups.
6. Have the class sing the song along with the tape.

Contributor

William Bickerdike is Senior Teacher at the British Council, Riyadh, Saudi Arabia.

Oral Directions

Levels
High beginning

Aims
Practice giving
comprehensible oral
directions,
understanding and
following directions,
and pronouncing
vocabulary words

Class Time
15 minutes

Preparation Time
None

Resources
None

This activity assesses oral comprehension through the use of total physical response (TPR) so as to lower the anxiety level of beginning language learners.

Procedure

1. Divide the class into two teams.
2. Ask the teams to line up opposite each other.
3. Have Student 1 in Team A give some simple instructions to Student 1 in Team B, such as "Put your pencil on the floor." If the student follows the instructions correctly, he gives instructions to Student 2 in Team A, who then gives instructions to Student 2 in Team B, and so forth. If the student does not follow the directions, he sits down and the next student has to try and follow the same instructions.
4. Pass down the line until everyone has had to follow some instruction. The last student in Team B gives the first person in Team A instructions.
5. See how many students in each team are still standing.

Caveats and Options

To control the instructions, make a set of cards with the instructions printed on them. Have the students take a card and read it aloud to the one following the instructions.

Contributor

Judi Braverman is an ESL teacher at Lidell School in Long Beach, New York, in the United States. She has trained ESL student teachers from Hofstra and Adelphi Universities.

Monday Morning Review Game

Levels
Beginning +

Aims
Review and reinforce
listening done
previously with a song
gap-fill
Practice segmenting the
components of long
stretches of speech

Class Time
30 minutes

Preparation Time
Minimal

Resources
Cassette player
Recorded song

Tape of a song based on gap-fill (cloze) exercises songs are popular with both teachers and students, but they are often used as a one-time Friday afternoon activity and left at that. Nation (1990) makes a strong case for the importance of review activities, and by doing another exercise with the song on Monday morning, students can acquire the elements on the threshold of learning rather than just pushing on to work with new material.

Whereas gap-fills often encourage students to focus their listening on individual words, this exercise encourages students to segment the words in longer stretches of speech. Normally this is very difficult for students because of the reduction and blending of sounds that takes place in English, but as they have previously done this song as a gap-fill, they have the aid of memory when doing this exercise.

Procedure

1. On the previous day students should have done a gap-fill with the song, with individual words or perhaps phrases blocked out. Students should also have completed a task that required them to read the lyrics, and discuss them, or at least have sung the song.
2. Tell the students you're going to play the whole song or a particular part and that they should completely reproduce what they hear. You will hear groans of resistance or perhaps disbelief because this will seem too difficult, and it probably is.
3. The key to making this exercise work is to turn it into a game. Put students in groups and tell them they will get one point for every word of the song they can write down. Tell them how many lines the song or section of the song has. Let them listen to the song a few more times.

4. To conclude, either compare the groups' final versions or have them write their version on the board, and count up the words. Give the group with the most correct words a big hand.

References and Further Reading

Nation, I. S. P. (1990). *Teaching and learning vocabulary*. New York: Newbury House.

Contributor

Eric Bray teaches at Kyoto YMCA English School in Japan.

Scrambled Song

Levels
Any

Aims
Practice dealing with
longer tracts of spoken
(i.e., sung) language
Recognize extended
discourse and
connecting words

Class Time
15–20 minutes

Preparation Time
20 minutes

Resources
Paper or index cards
Cassette player
Recorded song

Because music is a universally popular medium and songs often tell a story, a song is an excellent vehicle to show how sentences are connected using transition words, conjunctions, and adverbials. This activity can help students improve their discourse competency.

Procedure

1. Choose a song based on a structure (e.g., the simple past, the future, conditionals), a function (e.g., greeting and leave taking), a lexical field, melody, phonetics (e.g., /l/-/r/), or popularity with class members.
2. Write each line of the song on paper or cards.
3. Briefly tell the class the story line of the song and preteach any vocabulary that is critical for understanding the gist of the song.
4. Give each student a card with a line from the song. Start the tape and have the students put the lines in order by taping the cards on the board, forming a circle or line, or laying the card on a table or on the floor.
5. Play the song a second time, allowing students to switch the order of the cards. Alert students to connecting words and rhymes.

Caveats and Options

You could expand the story line in many different ways—for example, with discussion about the choice of words, symbolism, idiomatic expressions, stress and intonation, or discrimination of minimal pairs.

Contributor

Dennis Bricault teaches at North Park College, Chicago, Illinois, in the United States.

Students as Stars

Levels
Beginning–intermediate

Aims
Practice following instructions
Get to know each other

Class Time
25 minutes

Preparation Time
5–10 minutes

Resources
A list of instructions

Much of what is practiced in listening class is overheard speech (i.e., listening to people introduce themselves, listening to a person giving directions to another). In life, learners must understand what is said directly to them. This activity gives students a chance to respond personally in class.

Procedure

1. Before class, write out 8–10 sentences like the following:

   Write your hometown (or home country) in the square.
   Write your favorite kind of music in the circle.
   What school subject don't you like? Write it in the triangle.

2. In class, draw a number of shapes (e.g., stars, rectangles, circles) on the board, one for each sentence you have written. Preteach the names of the shapes if necessary. Have learners copy the shapes onto a sheet of paper.
3. Tell the students to listen to the sentences you say and answer for themselves. Note: They should not write the questions.
4. Read each sentence twice. The second time, you may want to rephrase the sentence (e.g., "Write a favorite free time activity in the second circle. In circle number two, write something you like to do.").
5. After the listening task is finished, have all the learners stand up, circulate and do a Find-someone-who activity based on the items (Find someone whose favorite free time activity is . . .). They write that person's name and answer next to their own. They change partners for each item.

Caveats and Options

The examples give are for high beginning students. For an intermediate class, you might want to use sentences with more complex structures.

Contributors

Steven Brown is Curriculum Coordinator at the University of Pittsburgh English Language Institute in the United States. Marc Helgesen is Associate Professor at Miyagi Gakuin Women's College, Sendai, Japan. They are coauthors of the Active Listening series (Cambridge University Press) and the New English Firsthand series (Longman/Lingual House).

A Joke a Day

Levels
High intermediate +

Aims
Focus attention at the beginning of a listening class
Experience a positive affective environment through the use of humor

Class Time
3–5 minutes

Preparation Time
5 minutes

Resources
Joke book

Students will expend great effort to understand a joke and will fully concentrate their listening ability to do so. Furthermore, they look forward to each day's jokes and tend to come to class on time so that they won't miss them. In fact, after you've established this joke-telling routine, if you forget to tell your jokes one day, they'll be sure to remind you. This activity will help you stay prepared.

Procedure

1. Explain that the activity is a warm-up for the more involved listening exercises to follow. Point out that while being entertained, the students are also being exposed to elements of English humor, an authentic cultural experience. And they might even learn a joke or two that they can tell later.
2. Read two or three jokes at the start of each class. Don't worry if the students don't understand and don't laugh, or if they do understand and groan. They will usually be amused just by your hopeful enthusiasm. You'll probably need to explain most of the jokes later, which, of course, kills the humor's impact but achieves one of the activity's aims of focusing students' attention.

Caveats and Options

1. Let any volunteers tell a joke they know. Just be sure it's clean first. Be sensitive to conservative cultural values that some in the class may hold.
2. Don't pitch this at too low or too serious a group.
3. Good joke books include those by noted Irish comedian, Hal Roach, and any of the many clever children's joke books currently available

(some surprisingly good ones exist). These two sources offer lots of usable material that is clean, amusing, and easily understood in terms of both vocabulary and culture.

Contributor

Joseph R. Fraher has an MA in TEF/SL from San Francisco State University. He currently teaches in Japan.

On Tour

Levels
Beginning–low
intermediate

Aims
Practice listening for
specific directions
Enjoy listening for
directions

Class Time
15 minutes

Preparation Time
5–10 minutes

Resources
Worksheet with place
names on it (see below)

Most textbooks deal with giving directions in a traditional way, that is, they use street maps. This activity makes giving directions more enjoyable by having as its product the drawing of an animal.

Procedure

1. Tell the students that they are going to trace the routes taken by two groups of tourists on an island.
2. Tell students that they don't have to listen to everything they hear. They only have to identify the place name and draw lines linking one place to the next.
3. Give out copies of the worksheet or write up the names in the design you want on the board. For example:

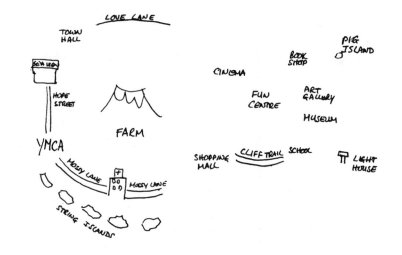

4. Tell the students that you will describe a day's outing of some tourists on this island. The students must listen to your story and draw a line showing the route that the tourists took on their tour. Then start telling a story similar to the following:

A group of tourists have come to visit this island. They are staying at the YMCA. Let's look for the YMCA. It's a little to the west of Mossy Lane, south of Hope Street. [Make sure everyone has found the place.] The tourists didn't know where to go. They had no guide, only a simple map, like the one you have. So they decided to walk south along Mossy Lane. They passed the hospital and reached the shopping mall. But soon, many of them were unhappy. Some wanted to do fun things. Others wanted to do serious things.. So they decided to go their different ways. The first group wanted to do serious things. From the shopping mall, they went west past the school to the museum.

Let's check. Have you drawn a line from the YMCA to the shopping mall, and then to the museum? Okay, let's see where they went to after the museum. Do you see an art gallery to the north of the museum?

5. Once you have given all the directions and the class has drawn lines between the places, ask them what they think the name of the island is. In the example here, it is, of course, Cat Island.

Caveats and Options

1. At the end of the activity, once the students have realized that they have drawn a cat, you can get them to work in groups to design a map themselves in the shape of an animal. Then they can work in pairs, giving directions for another student to follow.
2. I have tried this task with different learners of different ages, from children to 40-year-old adults, with enthusiastic responses. However, the style and language needs to vary with the learners.

Contributor

Hyacinth Gaudart is Associate Professor at the Faculty of Education, University of Malaya, Kuala Lumpur, Malaysia. She is the author of several textbooks and workbooks for adolescent learners in Malaysia.

Teaching Songs

Levels
Intermediate +

Aims
Learn language from
pop songs

Class Time
45 minutes–1 hour

Preparation Time
Varies

Resources
Cassette player
Recorded songs

Students usually enjoy this activity because they get to teach something themselves. It requires minimal preparation and enables students to learn language using pop songs. Songs sung at a moderate speed by an individual rather than a group work best.

Procedure

1. Invite your students to bring to class songs they would like to teach to the rest of the class (on tape, preferably with a copy of the lyrics). In general, only one student should be teaching at a time (although team teaching might work in some situations).
2. Meet with the students individually to go over the song they have selected (e.g., vocabulary, idioms, grammar, pronunciation). Make sure they understand the general meaning of the song as well as how they are going to teach it.
3. If you want to do an additional activity with the song in question, prepare appropriate questions or exercises (e.g. focusing on idioms, poetic devices, pronunciation or a relevant grammar point).
4. Make copies of the lyrics for the students, making sure to include the artist's name and, if possible, the year of the song.
5. On the day when the student is to teach the song, make sure the tape is cued. It is probably best if you operate the cassette player because the student who is teaching will be busy at the chalkboard.
6. Play the song once through for the class to hear.
7. Rewind and play the song a line at a time. Have the student-teacher elicit the words in each line from the class, drawing lines (as in a cloze exercise) and giving clues for words that are more difficult to hear.
8. Continue this way through the whole song.

9. Once you are finished, hand out copies of the lyrics and any additional exercises for the students to complete. Discuss the overall meaning of the song as well as any specific vocabulary that is still unclear, including idioms.
10. Finally, sing the song as a class.

Caveats and Options

References and Further Reading

For some great ideas on how to use songs in class, see Murphey (1992).

Murphey, T. (1992). *Music and song*. Oxford: Oxford University Press.

Contributors

Erica Hofmann and Mark Dickens teach at Fields College International, Victoria, Canada.

Partners

Levels
Any

Aims
Break the ice in a new class
Ask, listen to, and answer questions

Class Time
15 minutes/round

Preparation Time
Varies

Resources
Game show realia such as a microphone and music

Many students enjoy watching game shows on television. Putting this typical question-answer activity into that format can increase class interest.

Procedure

1. Assign partners. They should not know each other well.
2. Give the pairs 3-5 minutes to talk. Instruct them to learn as much about each other as possible. Give examples of questions they will be asked to answer later.
3. Have four pairs sit in front of the class, facing the other students.
4. Act as master of ceremonies. Have one student from each pair leave the room.
5. Ask each remaining partner three questions about the partner who has left. (e.g., "How long has your partner lived in this country?")
6. Ask the absent partners to return.
7. Ask the returned student the same questions their partners have just answered about them.
8. Have the other students (the audience) decide whether or not the answers match. Award each pair 5 points per matching answer.
9. Begin a new round with new pairs.
10. The class pair with the most points wins.

Caveats and Options

Allow the audience to write and ask the questions.

Contributors

Sally La Luzerne-Oi and Cindy McKeag Tsukamoto are coauthors of Tell Me About It, *an intermediate listening-speaking text (Heinle & Heinle). They currently teach in the United States, at Hawaii Pacific University and Roosevelt University, Illinois, respectively.*

Generating Language Through Song

Levels
Intermediate

Aims
Write words, phrases, and sentences heard from a recorded song
Learn the meaning of some new words through context
Answer specific questions
Answer a cloze test with 75% proficiency level

Class Time
45 minutes–1 hour

Preparation Time
45 minutes

Resources
Cassette player
Recorded song
Chalkboard (optional)

Procedure

1. Play the tape. Have the students listen to and write down any words, phrases, or sentences they hear from the tape.
2. Give each student a copy of the song, or post a copy of the song on the board for everyone to see.
3. Have the students compare their work with the copy of the song.
4. Ask a student to read the song aloud.
5. Ask the students to underline difficult words and phrases.
6. Go over the difficult words or phrases with the class focusing their attention on the context. Have them guess the meaning.
7. Ask a student/students to read the song again.
8. Ask several comprehension questions about the song.
9. Have the class sing the song together.
10. Hand out a cloze text of the song (try to predict what some of the difficulties will be and include them as part of the cloze) and have the students complete this either in class or as homework.

Contributor

Milagros Milan is an ESL Instructor at the Technodent Training Center, New York, in the United States.

Add to My Story

Levels
Low intermediate +

Aims
Memorize a story
Listen to conjunctions
Reconstruct a story

Class Time
30 minutes

Preparation Time
None

Resources
None

G amelike activities relax the class and aid comprehension.

Procedure

1. Create groups of eight and ask them to sit in a circle.
2. Tell the students that they are going to make up a story. Each student has to contribute a sentence in turn. To do this they have to listen to the previous sentences and the conjunction that precedes their turn. Tell the students that the stories must sound true and realistic and that the ending cannot be "then he woke up."
3. Inform the group that any student can begin the story and that the person on his/her right must continue it. Each students should think of a sentence but end with a conjunction so that the student that follows has to add to the idea.
4. Have the students not only say their own sentence but repeat all the preceding sentences. This way the story will be told many times. Ask the rest of the group to listen and make sure the same story is being told each time.
5. Circulate and help when necessary to get an idea how the stories are proceeding.
6. After 15 minutes tell the students that they have three more turns to finish their stories.
7. Ask one member of each group to stand up and retell the story to the class.

Contributor

Elizabeth A. Price is an EFL teacher with the British Council.

Addendum: Planning and Troubleshooting

Listening Comprehension in the ESOL Listening Curriculum: Program Review and Needs Analysis

Levels
Any

Aims
Learn about the listening skill-building curriculum, both the explicit listening instruction and the listening practice opportunities provided by the program
Provide information about students' listening needs

Class Time
Varies

Preparation Time
Varies

Resources
Secretarial support time
Questionnaire

Listening, the language skill used most in life, needs to be a central focus in the ESOL program. Yet in some programs the amount of curricular time devoted to substantial, goal-oriented work in listening skill building is limited. A review of the listening component in the curriculum and a survey of learner needs can be very helpful. Such a review can report on purposes, materials, and activities in these areas: the purpose of the assigned listening activities and tasks (i.e., what one thinks a sequence of listening activities and tasks is designed to do to facilitate the development of listening skills) (Morley, 1992), the nature of the listening tasks, and the amount of time devoted to different kinds of listening activities.

A program review can look at two important types of listening time available in the target language during daily school or institute hours:

- *exposure time*: the amount of time each day in which learners hear L2 within the educational institution in any and all contexts
- *instructional time*: the amount of time in which students are involved in specific listening-oriented instructional activities in the L2, including activities that provide explicit instruction in the development of listening strategies and extensive listening practice.

The questionnaire in the Appendix, which has been used for on-site program review and for both preservice teacher preparation course work and in-service workshops, is a guideline resource for a listening program review. The purpose of the review process is threefold: (a) to survey listening instruction in a program, (b) to consider possibilities for changing and adding listening activities, and (c) to analyze learners' listening needs.

Procedure

1. Modify the questionnaire provided here (see Appendix) so that it is appropriate to your situation.
2. Plan the review with teachers and administrators.
3. Follow up with an appropriate analysis and synthesis of the information obtained.
4. Take action in curriculum revision, as indicated.

Appendix: Program Review and Needs Analysis Questionnaire With a Focus on Listening

Part I. Student Profile and Program Profile

A. Identifying information

1. Students
   a. Age
   b. Proficiency level(s)
   c. Reason(s) for studying the target language
   d. Premium placed on good listening skills

2. Program
   a. Setting
   b. Length of courses
   c. Classes offered
   d. Time allocations

B. Teacher role and student role

1. Classroom interaction patterns
2. Kinds of learning activities
3. Methodologies used

Part II. Listening Opportunities Available in the Program

A. Exposure time in listening to the L2

1. Time in L2 classes
2. Time in content or subject matter classes

      3. Time in class projects, programs, assemblies, extracurricular activities

   B. Instructional time in listening to the L2

      1. Two-way listening activities (i.e., interactive listening)
        a. Listening classes
        b. Listening exercises
        c. Listening activities
        d. Listening purposes
        e. Amount of time allocated
        f. Means of assessment

      2. One-way listening activities (i.e., noninteractive listening)
        a. Invited visitor talks
        b. In-class use of recorded materials such as films, videotapes, audiotapes or records

      3. Language learning center (or language laboratory)
        a. Audio and video materials available
        b. Types of content/topics on tape, levels of difficulty
        (Specify whether laboratory use is assigned or free choice. Specify whether broadcast-style group listening or individual access and control are used.)

Part III. Listening Opportunities Available in the Community

   A. Two-way listening (i.e., interactional listening, bidirectional)

      1. Personal business transactions at/for
        a. Stores
        b. Restaurants
        c. Services for health care, travel, household needs

      2. Recreational transactions
        a. Sports
        b. Hobby groups
        c. Organizations

3. Educational transactions
   a. Community education night classes
   b. Free courses

4. Social transactions
   a. Activities such as parties, luncheons, dinners, receptions, etc.

5. Vocational/work-related transactions
   a. On-the-job interactions with speakers of the target language.

B. One-way listening (i.e., little or no interaction, unidirectional)

1. Recreational, educational, political, religious activities
   a. Movies, plays, musicals, rock concerts, lectures, public forum debates and discussion, open political meetings, religious services

2. Public access listening activities
   a. Availability of television broadcasts, radio broadcasts

3. Public announcements
   a. Public address announcements at work, at school, or in bus stations or airports
   b. Emergency messages
   c. Recorded telephone messages

Part IV. Listening Needs Analysis

A. Where? (settings and situations involving listening)

1. Situational listening needs: educational, vocational, social, recreational, political, religious
(Specify individual settings within these situations where listening is especially important.)

B. What types of listening-communication formats? (Richards, 1990)

1. Two-way and one-way listening
2. Transactional and interactional functions (Brown & Yule, 1983)

C. With whom?

1. Participants and their roles in the above settings (student/teacher, patient/doctor, customer/clerk, guest/host, employee/employer)

D. Why?

1. Listening and performing actions and operations
2. Listening and transferring information
3. Listening and solving problems
4. Listening, evaluating, and manipulating information
5. Interactive listening and negotiating meaning through questioning/answering routines
6. Listening for enjoyment, pleasure, and sociability. (Morley, 1991)

References and Further Reading

Brown, G., & Yule, G. (1983). *Discourse analysis.* Cambridge: Cambridge University Press.

Morley, J. (1991). Listening comprehension in second/foreign language instruction. In M. Celce-Murcia (Ed.), *Teaching English as a second or foreign language*, (2nd ed.) (pp. 81–106). New York: Newbury House.

Morley, J. (1992). Theory and practice in listening comprehension. In R. J. Courchene et al. (Eds.), *Comprehension-based second language teaching* (pp. 119–149). Ottawa, Canada: The University of Ottawa Press.

Richards, J. C. (1990). *The language teaching matrix: Designing instructional materials for teaching listening comprehension.* Cambridge: Cambridge University Press.

Contributor

Joan Morley is Professor in the Linguistics Program and the English Language Institute at the University of Michigan, Ann Arbor, in the United States. She is the author of many publications in the areas of aural comprehension, pronunciation, speaking skills, and English for academic purposes curriculum. She is Past President of TESOL and served on the TESOL Executive Board for 10 years.

Troubleshooting

Levels
Low intermediate–
intermediate

Aims
Be exposed to
troublesome phrases

Class Time
2–3 minutes

Preparation Time
None

Resources
Listening exercise
Audio or a video
cassette recorder

This activity allows teachers to do something about their students' problems instead of merely having the students do an exercise and receive scores. The benefits of this activity are that the teacher deals with listening problems as they arise and that it provides a direct motivation for students to repeatedly listen to problem phrases. This lessens the risk that the students will become bored and cease to concentrate in this intensive listening activity. The activity should not be done more than twice with any exercise as the type of intensive listening involved is extremely tiring.

Procedure

1. Check the students' responses to a listening task by eliciting the answers from the students around the class
2. When there are conflicting responses, write them on the board and label them (a), (b), (c), and so forth. The following example, taken from a lesson with low intermediate students, illustrates the process:

   The students have to fill in parts of a dialogue. In one part of the dialogue, they hear and have to write down, "Where are you from?" Some students report nothing, others note "Where", "Where from," "Where do you from?," "Where's do you from?," or "Where are you from?"

   Write on the board:

   a. do you

   Where   b. 's do you _____ from?

   c. are you

3. Ask the students to focus on the phrases on the board. Play the relevant section of the tape again and have the class vote for (a), (b), or (c), according to what they hear.

268

4. If the class is still divided over what they are hearing, play the tape again.
5. When a clear majority of the class is voting for the phrase that is actually on the tape—in the above instance, (c)—indicate the answer and play the section of the tape once or twice again so that the students who were not sure about what was on the tape can hear the phrase with greater certainty about what the sounds relate to at the lexical level.

Caveats and Options

1. Focus on meaning: Stop the activity when most of the students guess the speaker's meaning. This usually occurs when the most prominent words have been identified—in the above example, when *where* and *from* were identified. In such cases, explain to the students that English is a "telegraph language": The most important words in a message are generally easy to hear and the less important words are not spoken so clearly. Emphasize that they will generally be able to make sense of the message from the words they can hear most easily unless they are so worried about what they have not understood that they are not thinking about what they have comprehended.
2. Zero response: If the majority of the students cannot recognize any of the words in a fill-in-the-blanks or partial dictation exercise, put dashes on the board indicating the number of words. For instance, the case above, involving "Where are you from?" would lead to the following on the board:

_____ _____ _____ _____?

Encourage the students to report even parts of words that they understand, and build up the phrase in this way using repeated listenings. For instance, you might go from

Wh _____ _____ *f*? in the second listening to
Where _____ *you from*? in the third listening, and so on.

Contributor

Steve Tauroza is a Lecturer in TESL at the City University of Hong Kong. He has had an active interest in researching and teaching L2 listening comprehension since 1980.

Using Your Problems

Levels
High intermediate +

Aims
Prepare to use self-access listening materials

Class Time
5–10 minutes

Preparation Time
5–10 minutes

Resources
Using Your Problems handout (see Appendix)
Self-access listening materials and facilities for their use

The great value in students doing self-access listening work is that they can focus on and overcome their individual problems. They must read the handout for techniques concerning how to do this.

Procedure

1. Give the student the following handout to read for homework prior to their first self-access listening session.
2. At the beginning of the first session, emphasize the main points in the handout and deal with any questions arising from the handout.
3. In subsequent sessions, refer back to the handout and reiterate points according to the behavior to the students. For example, if the students are not making much use of the rewind buttons, remind them of the importance of focusing on the problems that emerge during the exercises; if the students forget to bring their dictionaries, point out the importance of doing so, and so on.

Caveats and Options

Tailor the handout to the particular students receiving it and the self access materials they will use. For instance, recommend a particular bilingual dictionary if the class all share the same Ll and/or comment on any problems in the materials they will use, for example, if there is a particular speaker with a highly unusual manner of speaking or a topic that contains a lot of extremely low frequency words.

Appendix: Using Your Problems Handout

Get Out of the Test Routine

Listening is rarely taught but frequently tested. Therefore, you may have formed the habit of treating listening exercises like tests; that is, you listen to a passage once or twice, you answer some questions, you mark your answers. This approach has some value because it gives you exposure to spoken English. However it does little to help you overcome the difficulties you had in answering the questions.

When working by yourself, you will have the chance to get out of the test routine. You will be able to focus on your difficulties so that they decrease. The following pages contain advice on how to do this. Read them carefully so that you can develop your ability to understand spoken English.

General Advice

While you are working with the self-access materials, you will realize that you have some comprehension problems. It is important that you try to overcome these problems or else you will have the same listening problems at the end of this module as you had at the start. Therefore, do not race through the materials. There will be no prize for the student who completes all the units first. In fact, we do not expect many students to complete all the units, but we do expect you to spend time dealing with problems that become obvious to you during the module.

Using the Materials

You should use the first lesson to become familiar with the different materials. After that, find a course that you are comfortable with and work through that course. Some materials are easier than others, for example, "Task Listening," "Listening Tasks," "Listening," "Learning to Listen," and Reasons for Listening" are easier than the other materials.

Vary the materials you use so that over a 2-week period, you do a mixture of easy and difficult exercises. The easy materials will allow you to listen to lots of spoken English as you will move quickly from one exercise to another. This broad exposure will help you comprehend more rapidly when you hear people talking about similar topics outside the classroom. The difficult materials will stretch your listening ability to new areas such as those related to new topics and new styles of speech.

Some people like to listen to a passage entirely before they go back and focus on phrases that they have not understood. Other people prefer to stop the tape as soon as they come across something they are not sure about. Do whatever you prefer (you will probably find that what you prefer depends on the passage you are listening to).

You should focus on problems that relate to the answers required by the exercises. If you try to focus on all of your problems, you may simply drown in a sea of incomprehension.

Useful Tools

Dictionaries

In order to overcome some of your problems, you will need a quick reference dictionary, for example, a good bilingual dictionary.

Replay/rewind buttons

You will also need to use the replay and the rewind buttons on your cassette player. Repeated listening to a phrase will help make that phrase a part of your listening vocabulary.

Dealing With Specific Problems

Words That Are Completely Unfamiliar

When you do not understand a phrase on the tape, rewind the tape, and replay the phrase on it several times. If you still cannot understand the phrase, use the transcript to find out what is being said. If you do not know the meaning of the words, then look them up in your dictionary.

After this, listen to the phrase again. In this way, you will experience how the sounds represent words. This technique will help you build up your listening vocabulary.

Words That You Know by Sight but not by Ear

Sometimes, when you have a problem, you will look at the transcript and realize that you know the words when you read them. This means that the words belong to your reading vocabulary but not to your listening vocabulary. Obviously, you cannot make the word part of your listening vocabulary just by reading it. You must rewind the tape and replay the phrase several times in order to help you get to know the words by ear in the same way that you know them by sight.

Other Problems Affecting Words and Phrases

Sometimes you might find that you have a problem with a phrase that you would normally recognize when it is spoken. In this case, check the transcript and see if the speaker hesitates just before or during the phrase. The following items can cause comprehension problems: *Er . . . er . . . and He . . . um. . . arrived late, She c-c-couldn't . . .*

Even though such features are common in spontaneous speech, they are very rare in the materials used to teach listening comprehension schools. Therefore, if you are not used to such sounds, you might think they indicate the beginning of a word. If you are having such comprehension problems in places where hesitations occur, use the repeat and rewind buttons to get familiar with the phrases containing the hesitations. You will not have problems with these sounds, if you have enough exposure to them.

Problems with an Entire Passage

The rapid rewind and replay technique is fine when you are dealing with problems that relate to just a group of words or a sentence. However, what do you do when an entire listening passage is too difficult, for example, when the speaker talks rather quickly or has an unfamiliar accent or an unusual manner of talking or the topic is something you have never come across before?

There are two possible solutions. You can turn to the script of the passage, read it and then put it away and listen to the passage. Alternatively, you can make your own cloze listening passage in the following manner:

- Turn to the script of the passage.
- Place two pencils side by side down the middle of the page (or else, if you do not have two pencils, fold a piece of paper in half and then in half again and then in half again. The paper should

now be about 2 centimeters (1 inch) wide. Place this down the middle of the page).

You should then read the parts of the script that are not blocked out and check the meaning of any unknown words in a dictionary. You should also try to guess the identity of the words that you cannot see. Then, when you listen to the passage while rereading the script, you can check whether your guesses were correct or not.

The Reason for Making a Cloze Passage

The idea is that the pencils or paper will block out some of the words on each line. The parts of the script that you can see will help you a lot when you listen to the passage on the tape. The parts of the script that you cannot see will make it necessary for you to really listen to what is on the tape.

If you can read everything while you listen, you will not listen so attentively to what you hear. This type of listening will not increase your listening ability so rapidly as will the cloze listening. With the cloze listening, the covered words ensure that you must listen fully to the passage. Therefore, whenever you want to look at the script while you listen to the tape, make a cloze passage out of the transcript. Do not just read the entire passage while you listen to it because you will not get so much benefit from the activity.

Remember to use the rapid rewind and replay buttons if you have a problem recognizing words when you are using the transcript.

Self-access learning allows you to work at your own speed. You have the time to deal with your specific listening problems unlike in a teacher-led lesson where the teacher only has time to focus on general problems. Use your problems, work on them, and you will find that they disappear.

Remember, if you race from one exercise to the next checking your score without rewinding the tape to check your problems, you will carry your problems with you from one exercise to the next. However, like everything in life, you need balance in the way that you deal with your problems. If you spend too long listening to words and phrases attentively, you will feel very tired. So, don't spend more than 5 or 10 minutes doing this and don't do it after every listening exercise. Sometimes you should just go on to the next passage or exercise.

Remember to use your teacher as a resource and consult her when your dictionary fails to clarify all the unclear points in a passage.

And remember, be patient and work steadily and you will steadily improve. With some of the authentic passages, you may feel that you have only islands of understanding in a sea of incomprehension. However, if you use the above techniques, you will find the scene changes to one where you have continents of comprehension dotted by lakes of confusion and, as you go, on practicing your listening, you will find the distance between such lakes grows greater and greater while the lakes grow smaller.

Contributor

Steve Tauroza is a Lecturer in TESL at the City University of Hong Kong. He has had an active interest in researching and teaching L2 listening comprehension since 1980.